DIRECTIONS IN DEVELOPMENT

Gender and Economic Growth in Uganda

Unleashing the Power of Women

Amanda Ellis,
Claire Manuel,
C. Mark Blackden

THE WORLD BANK

Cover image: Fabric design by Flotea Massawe, female entrepreneur.

ISBN-10: 0-8213-6384-0
ISBN-13: 978-0-8213-6384-3
eISBN: 0-8213-6385-9
DOI: 10.1596/978-0-8213-6384-3

Library of Congress Cataloging-in-Publication Data

Ellis, Amanda, 1962–
    Gender amd economic growth in Uganda : unleashing the power of women / Amanda Ellis, Claire Manuel, C. Mark Blackden.
        p. cm. — (Directions in development)
    Includes bibliographical references and index.
    ISBN 0-8213-6384-0
      1. Women in economic development—Uganda.   2. Sex discrimination against women— Uganda. 3. Investments, Foreign—Law and legislation—Uganda. 4. Women—Uganda—Economic conditions. 5. Uganda—Economic conditions—1979–   I. Manuel, Claire, 1962– II. Blackden, C. Mark, 1954– III. Title.   IV. Directions in development (Washington, D.C.)

    HQ1240.5.U33E57 2005
    338.96761'0082—dc22

                                                                    2005044984

Contents

Tables

Figures

Foreword

Women are already a powerful force for growth in Africa. They are economic actors: workers, property owners, and entrepreneurs. Recognizing this fact is the first step to ensuring that women have fair access to the labor market, enjoy full rights to own property, and do not face even greater barriers to doing business than men do.

The study that led to *Gender and Economic Growth in Uganda: Unleashing the Power of Women* was carried out at the request of the Minister of Finance, Planning and Economic Development for Uganda, because the government was concerned that the specific challenges facing women had not been fully addressed in existing work on Uganda's investment climate. This landmark report reflects the government of Uganda's concern that without the full economic contribution of both men and women, opportunities for job creation and economic growth are being missed. The findings of this report indicate the considerable potential for economic growth that exists if Uganda is to unleash the power of women and support their full economic participation in the private sector.

Gender and Economic Growth in Uganda assesses the legal and administrative barriers faced by women, as identified by the World Bank Group's Foreign Investment Advisory Service (FIAS) and the International Finance Corporation's (IFC) Gender-Entrepreneurship-Markets Unit. The structure of the report mirrors that of the FIAS 2003 Administrative Barriers to Investment Report and is designed to highlight the gender dimensions of that research to encourage further replication.

The primary analytical sources for the report were the World Bank's *Doing Business in 2005* (World Bank 2005a), the World Bank's Strategic Country Gender Assessment (World Bank 2005b) of Uganda, and the African Development Bank's Multi-Sector Country Gender Profile. This assessment was conducted in consultation with country office staff, client stakeholders, and other development partners. Field assessments and workshops were used to refine the draft.

Honorable Professor Ssemakula Kiwanuka, the Ugandan Minister of State for Investment, formally launched *Gender and Economic Growth in*

Uganda in May 2005 in Kampala, Uganda, in the presence of over 120 business women. A two-day workshop for key women's business and advocacy groups and government counterparts informed the participants about international best practices in public-private dialogue and advocacy. The workshop participants subsequently formed a Gender Coalition to design strategic action plans to take the report's recommendations forward.

As a direct outcome of the report, the Companies Act is being redrafted in line with international best practices, and the report's findings and recommendations have been included in the National Gender Strategy Action Plan 2005–2014 and in Uganda's Medium-Term Competitiveness Strategy 2005–2009.

The IFC is pleased to support the integration of gender issues into work on the investment climate and looks forward to this report's catalyzing greater attention to the productive role women play in private sector development.

Michael Klein
Vice President and IFC Chief Economist

Acknowledgments

This assessment was prepared by a team consisting of Amanda Ellis, Claire Manuel, and C. Mark Blackden, with support from Sarah Lubega and Mary Kusambiza.

We thank Jozefina Cutura for valuable work in drafting and finalizing the report.

Helpful comments were received from Gerry Finnegan of the International Labour Organization; Margaret Kakande of the Uganda Ministry of Finance, Planning, and Economic Development; Maggie Kigozi of the Uganda Investment Authority; Sarah Kitakule of Uganda Women Entrepreneurs Limited; Fiona MacCulloch of the Uganda Ministry of Finance Regulatory Best Practice Programme; Leila Mokadem of the African Development Bank; Vincent Palmade of the Foreign Investment Advisory Service; William Steel of the World Bank; and Richard Stern and Nigel Twose of the Foreign Investment Advisory Service.

The assessment draws on numerous interviews with public and private sector stakeholders. The important contributions to the report made by the Council for the Economic Empowerment of Women in Africa, lawyers, and the staff of the Ministry of Finance, Planning and Economic Development; the Ministry of Gender, Labor and Social Development; the Uganda Investment Authority; and the Justice, Law and Order Sector are appreciated. We are grateful for their comments and suggestions.

We thank the Private Sector Foundation Uganda for coordinating consultations with relevant private sector groups, including the Uganda Women Entrepreneurs Association Limited, the Uganda Investment Authority, the Women Entrepreneurs Network, and the Council for the Economic Empowerment of Women in Africa. For special contributions, we thank the Women Entrepreneurs Network, Africa Women Economic Policy Network, and the Association of Uganda Women Lawyers.

We would also like to thank Honorable Professor Ssemakula Kiwanuka, Uganda's Minister of State for Investment; Grace Yabrudy, World Bank Country Manager for Uganda; Dr. Maggie Kigozi, the Executive Director of the Uganda Investment Authority; and Nigel Twose of the Foreign Investment Advisory Service for their support throughout this project.

Finally, the team would like to acknowledge the participation of the Uganda Private Sector Donor Group and the Gender Donor Group. We also thank the representatives of the Gender Coalition for taking the report's recommendations forward.

Acronyms

AMFIU	Association of Micro Finance Institutions of Uganda
CADER	Center for Arbitration and Dispute Resolution
CEEWA-U	Council for the Economic Empowerment of Women in Africa-Uganda
FIAS	Foreign Investment Advisory Service
FIDA	Ugandan Association of Women Lawyers
IFC	International Finance Corporation
IICT	Inter-Institutional Committee on Trade
ILO	International Labour Organization
JLOS	Justice, Law and Order Sector
MDG	Millennium Development Goal
MFPED	Minister of Finance, Planning and Economic Development
NAADS	National Agricultural Advisory Services
NGO	nongovernmental organization
OECD	Organisation for Economic Co-operation and Development
PEAP	Poverty Eradication Action Plan
PSFU	Private Sector Foundation Uganda
RIA	Regulatory Impact Assessment
TEA	total entrepreneurial activity
UIA	Uganda Investment Authority
UMACIS	Uganda Manufacturing Association Consultancy and Information
UP3	Uganda Public-Private Partnership
URA	Uganda Revenue Authority
UWEAL	Uganda Women Entrepreneurs Association Limited
VAT	value-added tax
WEN	Women Entrepreneurs Network

Overview

Uganda is a leader in Sub-Saharan Africa in recognizing linkages between economic growth and gender issues. These linkages are critical for achieving a variety of development goals:

- *Meeting the Millennium Development Goals (MDGs).* While the third MDG relates specifically to promoting gender equality and empowering women, research indicates that gender equality is critical for achieving all the MDGs.
- *Attaining the Poverty Eradication Action Plan growth targets of 7 percent.* Unequal education and employment opportunities for women in Sub-Saharan Africa are estimated to have retarded annual per capita growth by 0.8 percentage points between 1960 and 1992. This is significant, as a boost of 0.8 percentage points per year would have doubled economic growth over the period. Applying these aggregate results to Uganda suggests that the country could gain as much as 2 percentage points of GDP growth a year by eliminating gender inequality (World Bank 2005b).
- *Reducing poverty.* Poverty in Uganda has a predominantly female face. Households headed by widows are particularly vulnerable to asset depletion and impoverishment. As the 2004 Poverty Eradication Action Plan notes, "It is now clear that removing constraints caused by HIV/AIDS, the environment and above all gender inequalities is key to achieving Uganda's poverty eradication goals" (Government of Uganda 2004c, p. 4).
- *Reversing the recent spike in inequality.* The percentage of Ugandans with income below the poverty line rose from 34 in 2000 to 38 in 2003 (World Bank 2005b). Removing the legal barriers that prevent women from participating more directly in monetized economic activity has significant implications for improving family welfare (Dollar and Gatti 1999).
- *Increasing agricultural productivity and strategic exports.* Almost 70 percent of the Ugandan labor force was employed in agriculture-related activities in 2003. Women provide the bulk of this labor, but they lack control over resources, especially land, and have little incentive to provide additional labor for cash crops, given the gender division of resources.

- *Reducing Uganda's very high fertility rate.* Gender inequality in employment, earnings, and bargaining power within families plays a significant role in keeping Uganda's fertility rates among the highest in the world. At current fertility rates, Uganda's population could reach 100 million by 2050.
- *Attaining Uganda's long-term vision of becoming a middle-income country.* Developed countries are increasingly recognizing and benefiting from the economic potential of providing a level playing field for women. In the United States, for example, with its Equal Credit Opportunity and Women's Business Ownership Acts, businesses owned by women generated $2.46 trillion in annual sales in 2004 and employed 19.1 million people—1 in 11 Americans (National Women's Business Council 2005).

This assessment considers the relationship between gender and economic growth in Uganda in the context of promoting women's participation in business and entrepreneurship. Men and women both play substantial, albeit different, economic roles in the Ugandan economy. Each contributes about 50 percent of GDP, and women represent 39 percent of businesses with registered premises (Government of Uganda 2002b). A growing body of microeconomic empirical evidence—and emerging macroeconomic analysis—shows that gender inequality directly and indirectly limits economic growth in Uganda. A recent World Bank study suggests that the country could gain as much as 2 percentage points of GDP growth a year by eliminating gender inequality (World Bank 2005b). The Government of Uganda's Poverty Eradication Action Plan 2004 indicates that a one-time benefit of up to 5 percent of GDP could be realized (World Bank 2005a). Labor and time constraints differentially affect women's and men's capacity to engage in business activity, with significant consequences for strategic exports. It is important for Uganda to unleash the full productive potential of female as well as male economic actors if it is to achieve high and sustained rates of pro-poor growth.

Most female workers in Uganda are either unpaid family farm workers or self-employed in the informal sector. Women account for 80 percent of all unpaid workers. Research suggests that Ugandan women are highly entrepreneurial, contribute significant amounts of labor to the Ugandan economy (much of it unpaid), and are extremely creditworthy. (World Bank 2005b; UPPAP 2002; Global Entrepreneurship Monitor 2003) What is constraining women from contributing more to private sector–led growth in Uganda?

Key Findings

Building on the findings of *Uganda: Administrative Barriers to Investment Update* (FIAS 2003), this assessment identifies specific legal and administrative barriers to investment that have a gender dimension. Key findings and recommendations include the following:

- Barriers to formalization of a business appear to have a disproportionate effect on women entrepreneurs, in some cases creating an absolute barrier to their ability to formalize their businesses. A more radical approach to deregulation and to reform of the Companies Act and Chattels Transfer Act than is currently being considered by the Law Reform Commission may therefore be required to facilitate the entry of women entrepreneurs into the formal economy.
- Land allocation practices are a fundamental constraint to women entrepreneurs, especially as they affect access to credit. While there is scope for amending the Land Act, the Succession Act, and the Divorce Act to give women enhanced rights over land, the key issue is the inability of many women to enforce the rights they have.
- Women face barriers in using nonland assets as collateral because of the undeveloped personal and moveable property securities law.
- Poor people in general, and women in particular, lack information about their legal rights and access to mechanisms to enforce them. Reliance on the Local Council Court system to resolve commercial disputes puts women at a particular disadvantage because of traditional attitudes and the application of customary law.

Reducing the cost of business registration and approvals

Formalizing a business is a critical step in facilitating business growth. Company formation is particularly important because the limited liability status of companies encourages risk taking, and the share structure facilitates the pooling of resources.

While the delays and costs of registration and licensing processes impose a burden on all businesses, there is emerging evidence from the Government of Uganda's Regulatory Best Practice Programme that such requirements impose a disproportionate burden on enterprises headed by women. Evidence suggests that women perceive the regulatory burden as greater than men do, that women are "time poor" and therefore less inclined to formalize their businesses, and that enterprises headed by women are much more likely to be subject to harassment and to pay bribes than businesses head by men. Women are seen as "soft targets." (figure 1).

A pilot project in Entebbe to simplify the trade licensing system suggests that women respond well to simplified, speedy procedures and will come into compliance once it becomes feasible for them to do so. It is therefore recommended that registration and licensing procedures in Uganda

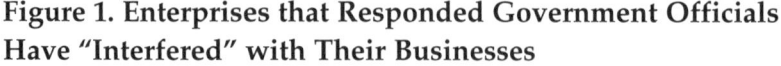

Figure 1. Enterprises that Responded Government Officials Have "Interfered" with Their Businesses

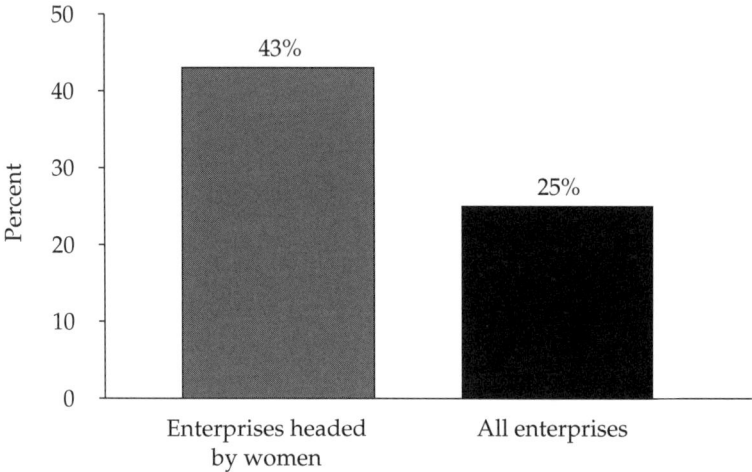

Source: Kirkpatrick and Lawson (2004).

be simplified in line with best practice in high-performing Commonwealth countries that originally had the same regime as Uganda.

Specific recommendations include the following:

- The blanket requirement for registering business names under the Business Names Registration Act, which applies to most unincorporated (and therefore micro and small businesses) should be abolished. International best practice requires prior approval for a business name only in restricted, defined circumstances.
- A more fundamental reform of Uganda's Companies Act should be undertaken than currently proposed in the Companies Bill. This should include the introduction of a simple registration form and the abolition of the requirement for lengthy memoranda and articles of association.
- The costly virtual monopoly of lawyers on company formation should be abolished.
- The Trade Licensing Act should be fundamentally reformed.

Increasing women's access to finance

A key constraint on businesses headed by women is the difficulty they face accessing finance. Although women make up nearly 40 percent of businesses with registered premises, they receive only 9 percent of all credit. Banks often require land as collateral, but as a result of land allocation practices that favor men, women hold only 7 percent of registered land in Uganda. Nonland securities law and practice is undeveloped in Uganda, particularly for micro and small businesses that are not registered as companies. The lack of credit information (such as that provided by a credit reference bureau) means that the excellent repayment rates by women in the microfinance system are not recognized.

Specific recommendations for increasing women's access to finance include the following:

- The ability of women to use nonland assets (such as stock or machinery) as collateral should be enhanced by putting in place a coherent legal framework for moveable personal property securities. The proposed Chattels Securities Bill is a step in the right direction, but it is flawed because it would allow for two concurrent registration regimes and a dual registration system.
- As a first step toward making credit information more accessible, the government should establish a publicly available register of judgment debts encompassing Magistrates and Local Council Courts.

Increasing women's access to land and site development

Land allocation practices operate as a fundamental constraint to women entrepreneurs, affecting not only their access to credit but also their ability to find business premises. Formal succession laws give women inheritance rights over land, but customary patrilineal practices (and the inability of many women to assert their legal rights) mean that formal legal provisions are rarely adhered to. Only about 15 percent of land is actively registered in Uganda, and it is rare for women to be registered as owners or for their rights to be noted on the register. A proposed amendment to the Land Act, contained in the Domestic Relations Bill, would make spouses automatic co-owners of family land. The Land Act gives some protection to spouses, requiring their consent before family land can be sold or mortgaged. Whether the act is enforced is in some doubt, however.

Specific recommendations for increasing women's access to land and site development include the following:

- More emphasis should be put on enabling women to assert their existing land rights when land is registered for the first time (under the Ministry of Water, Land and Environment's Systematic Demarcation Project, for example). If co-ownership is culturally unacceptable, one option would be for women to register a caveat on the title to protect their interest.

- The Registration of Titles Act should be reformed to create new modes of registration that protect a spouse's interest in the matrimonial home.
- The concept of giving a spouse a statutory life interest in the matrimonial home should be explored. This would chime with customary law provision for widows, unlike the automatic co-ownership proposal, which appears to conflict with cultural norms.
- Regulations should be developed to give more specificity to the duties of lenders and purchasers to obtain the consent of spouses to dispositions of family land.

Streamlining tax administration and customs

Women entrepreneurs face particular difficulties with taxes and customs. Recent evidence suggests that businesses headed by women are forced to pay significantly more bribes and are harassed more than businesses headed by men. Because Ugandan women tend to have less education and fewer formal business skills than men, they find it harder to deal with tax issues, and time-poor women find it difficult to comply with complex tax registration requirements. It is recommended that the Uganda Revenue Authority develop policies for assisting women entrepreneurs, through tax clinics and open discussions, for example.

Reforming labor laws

Fish processing and textiles and garments are among the sectors selected by the Government of Uganda as strategic exports. More than 30 percent of workers in fish factories are women, and women make up the vast majority of workers in garment factories. Improving working conditions for women would help increase output in these critical sectors.

Uganda's labor laws date from colonial times. They fail to address key issues for women workers, including discrimination, sexual harassment, and maternity leave and pay. Standards that are in place are not effectively enforced. Transparent and well-enforced labor standards would benefit both workers and investors.

Specific recommendation for reforming labor laws include the following:

- Bills should be prepared to enact health and safety standards to protect workers, provided such standards are affordable. Provisions that have proved controversial—such as maternity pay, which has been criticized as being unaffordable and potentially resulting in decreased employment opportunities for women—should be put off until a later stage.
- Realistic enforcement mechanisms should be put in place.

Increasing access to justice

Women lack information about their legal rights and access to mechanisms to enforce them. Reliance on the Local Council Court system to resolve commercial disputes puts women at a particular disadvantage because of traditional attitudes and the application of customary law.

Specific recommendations for increasing women's access to justice include the following:

- Women should be represented on the Commercial Court Users' Committee.
- The Justice, Law and Order Sector Gender Working Group should take an active role in developing the government's commercial justice reform agenda.
- Building on the 1998 Baseline Survey of Local Council Courts, follow-up monitoring and evaluation should be undertaken, in particular in relation to the effectiveness of new gender guidelines.
- Legal aid and paralegal projects should be enhanced to provide accessible advice for women operating businesses.
- Building on the civic education work undertaken through the Commercial Justice Reform Programme and by NGOs, further efforts should be made to give women practical guidance about their rights and how to enforce them.
- The Center for Arbitration and Dispute Resolution's work should be expanded to take on an outreach role, working with Local Council Courts to train their members in mediation techniques for commercial dispute resolution.

The Way Forward

The development of two key government programs—the Medium-Term Competitive Strategy (now known as the Uganda Public-Private Partnership, or UP3) and the commercial justice reform pillar of the Justice, Law and Order Sector—are entry points for implementing the recommendations of this assessment. Gender should be explicitly referenced in these strategies, and monitoring and evaluation should ensure that data are disaggregated by gender. The proposed introduction of Regulatory Impact Assessments represents an opportunity to include gender considerations in the policy- and lawmaking process.

The government should institutionalize women's active participation in public-private dialogue on private sector development issues. At least 30 percent of the members of economic advisory and political decisionmaking bodies (such as UP3 committees), should be women. The position for a

woman entrepreneur on the President's Investor Council should be institutionalized.

The Private Sector Foundation Uganda (PSFU) should establish a working group on women's entrepreneurship. Advocacy should focus on push-
ing for specific legal and regulatory reforms recommended in this assessment
through key entry points, including UP3 and the Commercial Justice Reform
Programme, and on influencing ongoing monitoring and evaluation
processes to ensure that data are disaggregated by gender.

Box 1. Matrix of Recommendations

A. Recommended Actions by the Government of Uganda

Issue	Recommendation	Impact/ suggested timing	Responsibility/ reform process
Business entry: registration and licenses			
Lengthy and complex business registration and licensing practices have disproportionately adverse effects on enterprises headed by women, often creating absolute barriers to formalization and growth. Current recommendations for reform do not address the issue adequately and are not in line with best practice legislative or procedural reform in Commonwealth countries (see World Bank 2005a for examples of procedural reform best practice).	Abolish blanket requirement for registration of business names under the Business Names Registration Act.	High/ immediate	Ministry of Justice and Constitutional Affairs (Commercial Justice Reform–JLOS)
	Fundamentally reform the Companies Act. Abolish the requirement for memoranda and articles and introduce a simple registration form.	High/ immediate	Ministry of Justice and Constitutional Affairs (Commercial Justice Reform–JLOS)
	Take forward administrative reforms of the Business Registry recommended in the 2003 FIAS report.	High/ immediate	Ministry of Justice and Constitutional Affairs, Business Registry (Commercial Justice Reform–JLOS)
	Fundamentally reform the Trade Licensing Act and the Local Government Reform Act to ensure equitable local taxation. Separate business licensing from revenue collection.	High/ immediate	Ministry of Local Government, Best Regulatory Practice Unit
	Abolish attorneys' virtual monopoly on the formation of companies (section 65 of the Advocates Act).	High/ immediate	Ministry of Justice and Constitutional Affairs (Commercial Justice Reform–JLOS)
Access to capital			
Lack of a coherent legislative framework for use of nonland assets (stock, machinery) as security combined with limited access to land by women means that many women lack collateral. Current proposals to reform the Chattels Transfer Act do not adequately address the issue.	Through the reform of the Chattels Transfer Act and Companies Act, introduce one unified, codified system for registering and recognizing nonland securities, including leases.	Moderate/ medium term	Ministry of Justice and Constitutional Affairs (Commercial Justice Reform–JLOS)
Obtaining access to credit information is very difficult. Women's excellent repayment rates in the microfinance system are not recognized.	As a first step toward making credit information more available, establish a publicly available register of judgment debts encompassing Magistrates and Local Council Courts.	High/ immediate	Judiciary (Commercial Justice Reform–JLOS)

(continued on the following page)

Box 1. (*continued*)

A. Recommended Actions by the Government of Uganda

Issue	Recommendation	Impact/ suggested timing	Responsibility/ reform process
Access to and control of land			
Land allocation practices hurt women, who are rarely registered on the title. Women's access to and control of land titles needs to be enhanced.	Encourage the citing of women's rights on titles during ongoing Systematic Demarcation Project.	High/ immediate	Ministry of Water, Lands and Environment (Land Sector Strategic Plan)
	Provide for co-ownership of matrimonial property through the proposed Domestic Relations Bill.	High/ medium term	Parliament
	Amend the Succession Act to provide for gender equality in succession.	Moderate/ medium term	Ministry of Justice
	Enact the Domestic Relations Bill provision for fair division of matrimonial property on divorce.	Moderate/ medium term	Parliament
Despite provisions under which a wife inherits 15 percent of matrimonial property upon the death of her husband, women are often dispossessed of their rights to matrimonial land upon divorce from or the death of their husbands and are not consulted about the disposition of family land.	Amend the Registration of Titles Act to create an appropriate form of registration to protect spouses' interest in land.	Moderate/ medium term	Ministry of Lands
	Develop regulations to make more specific the duties of lenders and purchasers to obtain consent of spouses to dispositions of matrimonial land.	Moderate/ immediate	Ministry of Lands
	Raise women's awareness of existing legal rights.	Moderate/ immediate	Ministry of Lands, JLOS, Ministry of Gender Labor and Social Development (Land Sector Strategic Plan)
	As a fallback, explore possible alternatives to statutory co-ownership (such as statutory life interest) proposed in the Domestic Relations Bill.	High/ immediate	Law Reform Commission

Box 1. (*continued*)

A. Recommended Actions by the Government of Uganda

Issue	Recommendation	Impact/ suggested timing	Responsibility/ reform process
Taxes			
Women, who tend to be less well educated than men and who are "time poor," find it difficult to comply with tax requirements and may be more subject than men to harassment and demands for bribes.	Develop policy and strategy for assisting businesswomen (by, for example, creating a women's desk, collecting gender-disaggregated data, establishing transparent guidelines, and conducting tax clinics and open discussions).	Moderate/ immediate	Uganda Revenue Authority
	Reform the Local Government Act to ensure a transparent system for taxation of businesses by local authorities.	High/ immediate	Ministry of Local Government
Labor laws			
Uganda's labor laws date from colonial times and are inappropriate for modern conditions. They do not satisfactorily address key issues for women workers—which international buyers view as critical competitive factors— including health and safety, discrimination, sexual harassment, and maternity leave.	Put in place realistic and affordable labor standards that will not make employing women unaffordable for businesses.	Moderate/ medium term	Ministry of Gender, Labor and Social Development
	Reform the Factories Act and related legislation to put in place and enforce realistic health and safety standards.	Moderate/ medium term	Ministry of Gender, Labor and Social Development

(*continued on the following page*)

Box 1. (*continued*)

A. Recommended Actions by the Government of Uganda

Issue	Recommendation	Impact/ suggested timing	Responsibility/ reform process
Access to justice			
Women have limited information about their legal rights and access to mechanisms to enforce them. Reliance on the Local Council Court system puts women at a particular disadvantage due to traditional attitudes and customary law applied in practice.	Have the Justice, Law and Order Sector Gender Working Group take an active role in developing the second phase of the Commercial Justice Reform Program.	High/ immediate	Commercial Justice Reform Program
	Building on the 1998 Baseline Survey of Local Council Courts, undertake follow-up monitoring and evaluation, in particular in relation to the effectiveness of new gender guidelines.	Moderate/ immediate	Ministry of Justice and Constitutional Affairs, JLOS Secretariat
	Building on the civic education work undertaken through the Commercial Justice Reform Program and by NGOs, give women practical guidance on their rights and how to enforce them (through radio soaps, information leaflets).	Moderate/ ongoing	Ministry of Justice and Constitutional Affairs, JLOS Secretariat, NGOs such as FIDA and CEEWA
	Expand the work of the Center for Arbitration and Dispute Resolution to outreach, working with Local Council Courts to train their members in gender-sensitive mediation techniques to resolve commercial disputes.	High/ immediate	CADER, Ministry of Local Government
Recent reforms to the Commercial Court have provided a flagship for reform. As plans are developed to roll out the reforms to the rest of the formal court system, gender issues should be central to the design.	Include women on the Commercial Court Users' Committee.	Low/ medium term	Commercial Justice Reform Program Ministry of Justice and Constitutional Affairs, JLOS Secretariat, Gender Working Group
	Involve the JLOS Gender Working Group in the design of the rollout phase of commercial court reform.	Moderate/ immediate	Commercial Justice Reform Program Ministry of Justice and Constitutional Affairs, JLOS Secretariat, Gender Working Group

Box 1. (*continued*)

A. Recommended Actions by the Government of Uganda

Issue	Recommendation	Impact/ suggested timing	Responsibility/ reform process
Public-private dialogue			
Women's active partici- pation in public-private dialogue on economic issues needs to be ensured, gender dimensions of private sector development need to be integrated into UP3, and gender needs to be included as part of the proposed Regulatory Impact Assessment process.	Introduce and institu- tionalize a minimum 30 percent represen- tation by women on economic advisory and political decision- making bodies, such as UP3 committees.	Moderate/ immediate	Ministry of Finance/Medium-Term Competitiveness Strategy Secretariat
	Institutionalize the position of a woman entrepreneur on the President's Investor Council.	Moderate/ medium term	Office of the President
	Allow CEEWA to join the Inter-Institutional Committee on Trade (IICT).	Low/ medium term	IICT, CEEWA
	Make sure that gender is explicitly referenced in the UP3 strategic plan, with gender- disaggregated monitoring and evaluation.	High/ immediate	Medium-Term Competitiveness Strategy Secretariat
	Ensure that the draft Cabinet paper on the introduction of Regula- tory Impact Assessments makes explicit reference to gender issues and that consideration of gender issues is part of the regulatory impact analysis process.	High/ immediate	Best Regulatory Practice Unit

(*continued on the following page*)

Box 1. (*continued*)

B. Recommended Advocacy Actions by the PSFU, Women's Business Associations, and NGOs

Issue	Recommendation	Impact/ suggested timing	Responsibility/ reform process
Gender dimensions need to be included in advocacy for private-sector policy development, reform, and implementation.	Include representative advocacy on key legal and regulatory reforms in the Gender and Growth Assessment. Key entry points include UP3 and the JLOS Commercial Justice Reform Program.	High/ immediate	PSFU, CEEWA, UWEAL, UIA WEN
	Ensure that monitoring and evaluation processes collect gender-disaggregated data.	High/ immediate	PSFU
Women face difficulty obtaining credit because of lack of collateral. Anecdotal evidence suggests that male credit officers discriminate against women. Women lack access to markets and training.	Increase awareness of women-friendly sources of capital (such as the Kikalu loan).	Moderate/ medium term	CEEWA, UWEAL
	Work with commercial banks to raise aware-ness of market oppor-tunities (an example is UWEAL's work with Barclays).	Moderate/ ongoing	UWEAL
	Enhance the provision of business develop-ment services and relevant technical training.	Moderate/ immediate	PSFU, with support from the World Bank, IFC, ILO, African Development Bank, and donors
Women have only limited knowledge of their legal rights, and women in business have only limited access to justice.	Enhance existing legal aid and paralegal projects to provide accessible advice specifically for business women.	Moderate/ immediate	Law Society Legal Aid, FIDA Uganda
	Undertake enhanced civic education programs for women on their legal rights and how to enforce them.	Moderate/ immediate	FIDA Uganda, with support from CEEWA
The ability of PSFU to advocate on behalf of women entrepreneurs needs to be enhanced.	Establish PSFU working group on women's entrepreneurship.	Moderate/ immediate	PSFU, support from CEEWA, UWEAL, and UIA WEN

1
Introduction

Women's entrepreneurship, the obstacles women face and the potential they offer to create both wealth and well-being are a worldwide phenomenon.
—Margaret Snyder, founder of the United Nations Development Fund for Women (UNIFEM)

This report examines legal and administrative barriers to domestic and foreign investment in Uganda that have a gender dimension. Building on the findings of *Uganda: Administrative Barriers to Investment Update* (FIAS 2003), the assessment includes additional, gender-related barriers to growth and investment. Addressing these issues represents a significant move toward creating an enabling environment for all businesses in Uganda and unlocking the economic potential of Uganda's women.

The report makes recommendations for gender-related legal and administrative reforms in the light of ongoing initiatives by the Government of Uganda. In addition to providing analysis and recommendations for Uganda, it develops an approach for growth and gender assessments that can be adopted in other countries.

The Legal Framework and Political Context for Gender Equality

Uganda's Constitution provides for equality between men and women and for affirmative action where such equality does not exist (box 1.1). The Constitution is in line with Uganda's commitments under the Convention on the Elimination of All Forms of Discrimination against Women, which Uganda ratified in 1985 without any reservations, as well as with other international obligations on gender equality.[1]

Box 1.1. Uganda's Constitution Provides for Equality between Men and Women

Various sections of Uganda's Constitutions ban sex discrimination, guarantee gender equality, and mandate affirmative action in favor of women who were marginalized because of their gender.

"The State shall recognize the significant role that women play in society." (National Objectives and Directive Principles of State Policy No. XV)

"… a person shall not be discriminated against on the ground of sex…." (Article 21(2)).

"...the State shall take affirmative action in favor of groups marginalized on the basis of gender… for the purpose of redressing imbalances which exist against them." (Article 32(1))

"1. Women shall be accorded full and equal dignity of the person with men.
2. The State shall provide the facilities and opportunities necessary to enhance the welfare of women to enable them to realize their full potential and advancement.
3. The State shall protect women and their rights, taking into account their unique status and natural maternal functions in society.
4. Women shall have the right to equal treatment with men … rights shall include equal opportunities in political, economic and social activities.
5. Women shall have the right to affirmative action for the purpose of redressing the imbalances created by history, tradition and custom.
6. Laws, cultures, customs or traditions which are against the dignity, welfare or interest of women or which undermine their status are prohibited by this Constitution." (Article 33)

Despite Uganda's Constitution, Key Legislation in Uganda Is Inconsistent with Gender Equality

The government has begun to create mechanisms to operationalize its international and constitutional obligations, including through the National Gender Policy (1997) (currently being revised) and the National Action

Plan on Women 1999.[2] Much remains to be done to take forward activities to implement gender equality in Uganda's legal framework, however. A key issue is the need to reform legislation that is unconstitutional because it discriminates on the basis of gender (box 1.2). The proposed Domestic Relations Bill, currently before Parliament, would go a long way to addressing these issues. In addition, Uganda needs to enact legislation that would address key social issues that affect gender relations and women's position in society and the home.

Enacting laws to implement Uganda's constitutional commitment to gender equality is important for growth. Some of the laws currently under consideration directly address women's ability to access economic assets

---

Box 1.2. Many Laws Require Amendment or Enactment to Address Gender Inequality in Uganda

Divorce Act

The Divorce Act lays down unequal standards for men and women. When a woman seeks a divorce, she must prove that her husband both committed adultery and either deserted her, was cruel to her, or failed to maintain her. In contrast, a man needs to prove only adultery to obtain a divorce.

In a case recently brought by the Strategic Litigation Coalition (*Uganda Association of Women Lawyers & Orgs v. Attorney General Constitutional Petition No. 2 of 2003*), Uganda's Constitutional Court declared these aspects of the Act to be unconstitutional under Article 2(2), which states, "If any other law or custom is inconsistent with any of the provisions of this Constitution, the Constitution shall prevail, and that other law or custom shall, to the extent of the inconsistency, be void."

Inequalities also exist in the division of assets on divorce. When a wife seeks a claim to marital property that was not directly acquired during her marriage, she is often deemed to lack legal and equitable rights. The wife's contributions to the home during the marriage are nonmonetized and usually not taken into account (Banenya 2002).

Domestic Relations Bill

The Domestic Relations Bill reforms and consolidates all laws relating to marriage, separation, and divorce, including by addressing the unconstitutional issues in the current Divorce Act. The bill:

- recognizes the principles of equality
- recognizes monogamous and polygamous marriage

(*continued on the following page*)

Box 1.2. (*continued*)

- sets out the rights and obligations in a marriage, providing for equal rights and making it an offence for one spouse to force the other to have sex
- bans widow inheritance (the custom in which a relative of the deceased husband inherits the widow as his wife)
- recognizes matrimonial property, recognizes the contributions of a wife to matrimonial property, and provides that such property is owned in common in undivided shares
- reforms divorce law, providing for the same grounds for divorce for men and women.

The bill, especially the provisions relating to co-ownership of matrimonial property, including customary land, is highly controversial. It is currently being considered by the Parliamentary and Legal Affairs Committee.

Succession (Amendment) Bill
The Succession Bill, prepared by the Uganda Law Reform Commission, would entitle a widow to half of the matrimonial home and other assets on the death of her husband. Under the current Succession Act, a wife is entitled to only 15 percent of these assets; if there is more than one widow, they share the entitlement.

Domestic Violence Bill
The Uganda Law Reform Commission is currently examining the nature and extent of domestic violence, victims and perpetrators, and causes and possible interventions in order to propose a domestic violence law.

(especially land) upon divorce from or the death of their husbands. Legislation directed at domestic relations between men and women can also affect women's ability to participate in the public and economic sphere. It can lead the way in changing social attitudes.[3] Legislation directed at social and family issues can have a direct impact on the economic empowerment of women. Uganda's 1996 Children Statute, for example, provides that both parents must contribute financially to the upkeep of their children and enables women to obtain this financial support when it is not provided. At least one legal aid clinic uses this legislation to encourage women seeking child maintenance to draw up a business plan and then encourage the father of the child to make a one-time lump sum payment to fulfill his obligations under the statute, thus enabling the woman to start a business.

Legislative Reform Is not Enough—Land Allocation Practices also Need Changing

The legal framework has a key role to play in determining women's access to key economic resources, including credit, land, and property. But legislative reform alone will not be sufficient. Uganda's land law is not discriminatory, but it does not address the highly unequal allocation of land between men and women in Uganda or ongoing inheritance and ownership practices that perpetuate this inequality (see chapter 4). The main issue is not legislative reform but changes in customary practice and attitudes.

It is not only Uganda's legislative framework and inheritance and ownership practices that limit women's access to economic resources. A perhaps more important issue is the fact that Uganda's population remains largely unaware of its legal rights or how to enforce them. This is especially true for women, who have even less access than men to legal advice and representation (Government of Uganda 2002a). (This issue is explored in chapter 7.)

Women are represented at every political level in Uganda, from local government, where one of every three councilors is a woman, to the national Parliament. This significant political progress has not been matched in the economic domain, however.

Culture Change Is Needed, Too

Reforming the law, working to change land allocation practices, and enhancing access to justice are clearly part of the solution to releasing the economic power of women in Uganda. However, culture also has a part to play. Ugandan lawyer Sarah Lubega (2000) suggests that the traditional concept of women in Uganda places them in an inferior position in relation to men. The assumption that a woman cannot do what a man can do is entrenched by traditional customs and norms in Uganda (box 1.3).

Box 1.3. Traditional Proverbs Suggest the Inferior Status of Women in Uganda

"When a woman assumes power in the house, the house is as good as destroyed because all sorts of people will seize the opportunity to confuse it." (Kiswahili)

"The woman grinds the flour but doesn't decide which ox shall be slaughtered." (Runyankole/ Rukiga)

Evidence from the Uganda Participatory Poverty Assessment Process/Participatory Poverty Assessment 2 illustrates how these attitudes can marginalize women as economic actors:

• Women often lack a voice in decisionmaking in the household as well as in the public sphere.
• Women often lack control over income, even when they provided the labor for it. Women lack incentives to raise cash crops, because men tend to control the resulting income (World Bank 2005b).
• Despite the introduction of universal primary education in Uganda, girls may not receive the same educational opportunities as boys.

Some practices that are justified as cultural and customary pose a threat to women's safety and security and limit access to justice.[4] Examples include female genital mutilation, early marriage, widow inheritance, the practice of grabbing property from widows and orphans, and domestic violence, which affects 40–45 percent of marriages. Female genital mutilation is an important issue for women in Uganda, who are both victims and perpetrators of the practice. One way of addressing the issue is to enable the women who perform the procedure to find alternative sources of employment.

Culture has a pervasive impact on social and economic life (table 1.1). It is a cross-sectoral issue that influences the roles and status of men and women in different sectors. The allocation of resources, decisionmaking power, status, opportunities, and rewards to men and women is largely defined by cultural norms, expectations, attitudes, and beliefs.

Many of the issues of power and control over assets highlighted in the Strategic Country Gender Assessment have cultural roots (table 1.2).

Many sources confirm the importance of bride price in defining a woman's place and value in society and the extent to which women control assets and resources (box 1.4). The proposed Domestic Relations Bill, currently before the Parliament, would ban payments for brides.

Cultural factors inhibit Ugandan women from realizing their potential in business. A woman involved in business is frequently referred to as an immoral person (Lubega 2000). A married woman usually must seek permission from her husband to conduct business, and particularly in rural areas women frequently have to give up income from their businesses to their husbands.

The imbalance between men's and women's rights in Uganda goes beyond the legal emancipation of women. Complex social, cultural, and political issues are at work (box 1.5).

Table 1.1. Effects of Selected Cultural Practices on Poverty in Uganda

Practice	Influence on gender dimensions of poverty
Payment of bride wealth	A woman's time and labor are considered part of the value received by her husband and his extended family. Practice predisposes girls to early marriage, which negatively affects their education opportunities and compromises their health and employment.
Domestic violence	Practice disempowers women and negatively affects women's health and productivity, sometimes resulting in death.
Widow inheritance	Practice disempowers women and may entail dispossession of property and children, especially girls. It predisposes women to HIV/AIDS, reducing the scope for protecting children.
Polygamy	Practice fragments land and makes it difficult for men to provide for their families. Women in polygamous marriages end up as family heads with limited resources, sharing scarce resources across many households. Fertility rates are higher among women in polygamous families, who compete for male heirs.
Female genital mutilation	Practice endangers the health of girls and women, increases the rate of maternal mortality, causes girls to drop out of school, strips women of their dignity, and creates trauma.
Inheritance practices	Practices perpetuate landlessness; attach a low value to women, who are rootless and visitors in their own homes; and reduce the potential productivity of women.

Source: Mukasa and others (2004).

The Economic Dependence of Women Lies at the Heart of the Problem

Women's lack of control over productive resources and assets is a systemic issue; inequity in marital status and property ownership intersects with cultural attitudes and beliefs to create formidable obstacles to change. The imperative to control women—embodied in the question "how can property own property?"—is underpinned by the fear that women will become promiscuous and indulge in extramarital affairs if allowed to work. Men express the view that women will become "uncontrollable," "unmanageable," "unruly," or disrespect men if they gain economic independence. They fear that allowing women to work may lead to family breakup, because women will be able to abandon their husbands once they are not economically dependent on them.

Table 1.2. Culture and Gender Disparities in Poverty Determinants in Uganda

Poverty determinant	Women (%)	Men (%)	Influence of culture
Ownership of registered land	7	93	Women are economically dependent on men. Land inheritance is mainly patrilineal.
Formal labor force participation	12	88	Women work largely at home and have limited job opportunities. No emphasis is placed on preparing them for the workplace. Training is often skewed toward culturally appropriate fields, regardless of their income-earning potential.
Wages of less than 40,000 USh a month	51	44	Less value is placed on women's work.
Literacy rates among people 10 and older	63	77	Literacy rates reflect the low value placed on the role of women outside the home. Grooming of women for marriage is a factor in limiting schooling and therefore literacy. Gender allocation of roles also affects girls' progression in formal education, the main channel for literacy.
Share of total enrollment at tertiary level	38	62	Poverty interacts with negative attitudes about girls' education. For many, investment in girls' education is an investment in the family or clan of the girl's husband or father. Early marriage also keeps tertiary enrollments low.
Maternal mortality ratio (per 100,000 live births)	506	n.a.	Women have no control over sexuality and resources, limited access to information. Harmful practices and taboos against women and children as well as early marriage contribute to high maternal mortality rates.
Distribution of credit	9	91	Lack of credit limits women's economic independence and affects gender relations.
People living with HIV/AIDS	51	49	Women have no control over their sexuality or bodies.
Likelihood of adults being sick within households	32	24	Women are exposed to heavier workloads and face exposure to hazardous conditions.

Table 1.2. (*continued*)

Poverty determinant	Women (%)	Men (%)	Influence of culture
Membership in Parliament and participation in governance and development structures	24	76	Leadership is the preserve of men. Women are not socialized to play political roles, have limited skills, and are not highly valued.
Chairperson of district land boards	4	96	Women have limited participation in governance structures. Ownership of land and participation in public life are male preserves.
Applications for processing land certificate titles	6	94	Applying for a land title is costly. Women lack exposure to land issues, have limited opportunity to inherit, are subject to land grabbing when widowed, and have limited knowledge of land rights and information on procedures.

Source: Mukasa and others (2004).

n.a. Not applicable.

Box 1.4. Payments for Brides Confirm Women's Status as Property

Bridewealth payments lead to the perception among both men and women that men own women and that it is therefore a women's job to both provide for and serve men. In a discussion of men's assets in Kigusa in Bugiri, one woman expressed a common sentiment when she said, "I was bought by the man, so my body is his asset to use as he wishes."

Bride price is also used to legitimize domestic violence. In a discussion of domestic violence in Katebe, Rakai, a male participant commented, "If you buy a cloth, do you not wash it any time you want?" The women agreed that as men had paid cows for them, they were property to be used as the men wish.

According to Human Rights Watch, bride price was once a gesture of appreciation to the bride's family; now men literally purchase their wives. As in a commercial transaction, the husband's payment entitles him to full ownership rights over his acquisition.

Source: UPPAP (2002); Human Rights Watch (2003b).

Box 1.5. Ugandans' View of Gender Relations and Legal Rights Vary

Both women and men note that "women have grown wings" and that "women's rights have become excessive, there is need to scale them down" (Baseline Study on Local Council Court 1998).

"Women were in support of the gender movement, while men saw it as a threat to their natural position in society and added that this gender movement posed a big threat to the institution of marriage" (Banenya 2002, p.17).

"In urban centers, a recent practice has developed of giving very generous wedding gifts to the bride, including furniture and appliances. This is said to be changing the balance of power in the home, with men being uncomfortable with the matrimonial home being furnished through the woman" (discussion with woman lawyer in Kampala, November 2004).

The law on defilement (contained in the Penal Code), which makes having sexual relations with a girl under 18 a capital offence, has been seen as discriminatory against men and boys. It does not address the issue of boys who are victims of sexual abuse nor can women be prosecuted under it (although there are plans to amend the law to address these issues). Moreover, the law is perceived as having used to victimize men by accusing them of defilement and then demanding bribes to drop charges (The New Vision, November 19, 2004, and discussions with lawyer in Kampala, November 2004).

Women who are allowed to work face different problems. According to the Uganda Participatory Poverty Assessment Process/Participatory Poverty Assessment 2, when a husband learns that his wife can earn income, he swiftly shifts the burden of looking after the family to her. Women are left to shoulder the responsibility of caring for the home, paying school fees, paying medical bills, buying food and clothes for the entire family, ensuring provision of all household necessities, and paying taxes for their husbands.

Cultural imperatives often drive women to support and uphold these views themselves. One woman argued that "at times, we women are a problem because after our husbands have supported us to do business, when we become successful we end up despising them" (UPPAP 2002).

Interviews conducted with women entrepreneurs in November 2004 reinforced the centrality of these culturally based obstacles to women's economic empowerment. While access to finance and the need for management training and other business development services emerged as key issues, the reluctance of husbands to allow their wives to engage in business activity was never far from the surface. As a consequence, women's enterprises often remain precarious, usually tied to small-scale and informal activities that can be reconciled with their domestic responsibilities. This means that a substantial segment of Uganda's entrepreneurial spirit remains underutilized and is unable to realize its full potential in contributing to the country's growth and economic dynamism.

Lack of access to business development services and training, particularly in financial management and exporting, were cited as constraints to female entrepreneurial development. These issues are addressed in depth in the Integrated Framework of the African Development Bank and the International Labour Organization, which addresses the enabling environment for growth-oriented women entrepreneurs.

Initiatives to Address Growth and Gender Issues

Some encouraging initiatives are underway in Uganda to address gender imbalances in economic empowerment. Women's business associations have undertaken advocacy, networking, and training initiatives. The recent government initiative to integrate entrepreneurship courses into the educational curriculum is laudable and should help mitigate the negative attitudes that women entrepreneurs believe currently affect their business operations. The Uganda Investment Authority encourages positive role models through the Distinguished Woman Investor of the Year Award at its annual awards ceremony.

Uganda: Administrative Barriers to Investment Update (FIAS 2003) reviewed the legal framework for business and foreign investment in Uganda. It identified administrative barriers to establishing, locating, and operating a business and made recommendations for streamlining and simplifying administrative procedures. It also considered administrative barriers in three of the sectors targeted for increased investment: textiles and apparel, fisheries, and coffee. Key barriers to investment identified in the report include corruption, lack of consistency between laws and procedures on the books and actual procedures, cumbersome and costly mechanisms for payments of fees for administrative transactions, decentralization, multiple licensing, and poor coordination between authorities.

This assessment revisits some of these issues in the light of the issues outlined above. It highlights legal and administrative barriers that have a disproportionately negative effect on businesses headed by women. It suggests that when legal and administrative barriers to investment are viewed through a gender lens, new issues come into focus and priorities may need to be reconsidered. Key findings and recommendations include the following:

- Barriers to formalization of a business may have a disproportionate effect on women, in some cases making it impossible for them to formalize their businesses. A more radical approach to deregulation, in line with global best practice, is recommended to encourage women entrepreneurs to enter the formal economy. Recommended measures include the legislative reforms discussed in this assessment and the administrative reforms described in *Doing Business 2005* (World Bank 2005a).

- Land allocation practices operate as a fundamental constraint to women entrepreneurs, especially in relation to access to credit. While there is scope for amending the Land Act, the Succession Act, and the Divorce Act to give women enhanced rights over land, the inability of many women to enforce even the rights they currently have is a critical issue.
- It is difficult for women to access formal sources of credit by using non-land assets as collateral because of the undeveloped system of personal and moveable property securities law.
- Poor people in general, and women in particular, lack information about their legal rights and access to mechanisms to enforce them. Reliance on the Local Council Court system for commercial dispute resolution puts women at a particular disadvantage, because traditional attitudes and customary law are applied.

The rest of this assessment is organized as follows. Chapter 2 examines the linkages between gender, growth, and poverty. Chapters 3, 4, and 5 focus on legal and administrative barriers that impede women's ability to establish a business, locate it, and operate it. Chapter 6 considers specific issues that constrain women's ability fully to participate in key sectors of the Ugandan economy. Chapter 7 examines the vital issue of access to commercial justice. Chapter 8 assesses entry points for reform.

Notes

1. Article 15 of the Constitution provides for equality between men and women before the law and in civil matters. Uganda is also a signatory to the Universal Declaration of Human Rights, the International Covenant on Civil and Political Rights, the International Convention on Economic, Social and Cultural Rights, the African Charter on Human and People's Rights, and the Beijing Declaration and Platform for Action.

2. The Plan was the result of a consultative process that sought to implement the commitments made by the Government of Uganda at the 1995 Fourth World Conference on Women in Beijing. The Plan identifies four critical areas of concern for Uganda: poverty, reproductive health and rights, legal framework and decisionmaking, and the education of girls. Strategic objectives, actions, indicators, and actors are identified for each priority area.

3. Legislation passed in the United Kingdom in the 1970s is viewed as having been key in changing attitudes toward race relations and equal opportunities there.

4. This section draws on Mukasa and others (2004), in particular chapter 10.

2

How Are Growth and Gender Linked?

It is now clear that removing constraints caused by HIV/AIDS, environment and above all gender inequalities is key to achieving Uganda's poverty eradication goals.
      —Poverty Eradication Action Plan 2004/05–2007/08

This chapter addresses the linkages between gender and growth in Uganda in the context of efforts to promote entrepreneurship and develop women's businesses.[1] Both men and women play substantial (though different) roles in the Ugandan economy and household, and there is a growing body of microeconomic empirical evidence—and emerging macroeconomic analysis—indicating that gender inequality directly and indirectly limits economic growth, principally through gender differences in economic options, incentives, and productivity. Some of this evidence comes from Uganda and elsewhere in Sub-Saharan Africa. Awareness of the importance of gender in the development agenda has grown considerably, bolstered by mounting evidence of the costs of gender inequality for development and greater recognition of the need to address gender to ensure development effectiveness.

The Roles of Men and Women in the Ugandan Economy

A distinguishing characteristic of Uganda's economy, which it shares with other Sub-Saharan African economies, is that both men and women play substantial economic roles. Although the economy has diminished its dependence on agriculture, the sector still contributes almost 40 percent of GDP, 85 percent of export earnings, and 80 percent of total employment (Moncrieffe 2003).

One way to capture the dynamics of the different contributions of men and women to the productive economy is by looking at the "gender intensity of production" of different sectors, an approach developed by Elson and Evers (1997) (table 2.1). Their estimates, while highly aggregated, provide a useful indication of the magnitude of the contributions of men and women to the economy. These estimates show that women represent the majority of the labor force in agriculture in Uganda, while men represent a much larger majority of the labor force in industry and services. Men and women each contribute about half of Uganda's national product. These estimates probably understate women's contribution to the economy, although they do not take account of gender differences in productivity.

Micro-level country data confirm the general validity of these aggregate estimates. About 86 percent of the population lives in rural areas, and 77 percent of the active labor force in rural areas is employed in agriculture (Government of Uganda 2004c).

The vast majority of women work in agricultural subsistence work, particularly crop production (60 percent of women list "cropping" as their occupation, as opposed to only 49 percent of men) (Lawson 2003). Women are more active than men in agriculture, particularly in food crop production, marketing, and processing of agricultural products (table 2.2). This gender division is confirmed by the National Agricultural Advisory Services

Table 2.1. Structure of Uganda's Productive Economy, by Sector and Gender, 1997 (percent)

Sector	Share of GDP	Gender intensity of production		Contribution to GDP	
		Women	Men	Women	Men
Agriculture	49.0	75	25	72.6	24.8
without smallholder sector	33.0	80	20	—	—
Traditional exports	3.5	60	40	—	—
Nontraditional agricultural exports	1.0	80	20	—	—
Industry	14.4	15	85	4.3	24.8
without manufacturing	6.8	—	—	—	—
Services	36.6	32	68	23.1	50.4
Economy as a whole	100.0	50.6	49.4	100.0	100.0

Sources: Share of GDP and gender intensity of production are from Elson and Evers (1997). Contributions to GDP by sector and by gender are from the Africa Country Gender Database and World Bank estimates. Estimates for the economy as a whole are based on World Bank calculations.

Table 2.2. Contributions to Production and Ownership of Land by Men and Women in Uganda (percent)

Indicator	Women	Men
Population	51	49
Food production	80	20
Planting	60	40
Weeding	70	30
Harvesting	60	40
Processing/preparation	90	10
Access to and ownership of land and related means of production	8	92

Source: Akello (2001).

Note: Estimates are preliminary.

(NAADS) strategy, which notes that women play a pivotal role in agriculture in Uganda, providing most of the labor force. Men and women have distinct roles within the farming systems, as they are engaged in the production of different crops and livestock. Men tend to concentrate on the production of cash crops (coffee, cotton, tobacco, and lately cereal production for the market), while women concentrate on the production of food crops, mainly for family consumption, while simultaneously providing much of the labor for cash crop production. In livestock production, women concentrate on poultry and small ruminants (mainly rabbits, pigs, goats, and sheep), while men concentrate on large stock (mainly cattle) (NAADS Secretariat 2003).

In nonfarm production, men predominate in the formal economy, where they represent 61 percent of employees (Uganda Bureau of Statistics 2003), while most women workers are self-employed or work as unpaid family workers (Government of Uganda 2003b). Women represent nearly 40 percent of business owners with registered premises in the Uganda Business Register, but these businesses are more likely than those owned by men to be informal microenterprises with a small number of employees (Government of Uganda 2003b). When rural women have the opportunity to do so, they take the chance to increase their incomes through nonfarm activity (box 2.1) (Canagarajah and Bhattamishra 2004).

A global study of entrepreneurship suggests that Uganda has an exceptionally high level of entrepreneurial activity (Global Entrepreneurship Monitor 2003). According to this study, in 2003 Uganda had the highest total entrepreneurial activity (TEA) index (29.2) among all countries surveyed. This means that 29 out of 100 Ugandans were engaged in some kind

---

Box 2.1. Nonfarm Employment Helps Ugandan Women Rise from Poverty

Household data show that nonfarm employment is an important source of growth in Sub-Saharan Africa. Women's labor force participation in the rural nonfarm sector increased between 1992 and 1996, raising the incomes of women and of households headed by them and reducing poverty. When provided with the opportunity, women are able to participate and to contribute to economic growth and poverty reduction. Removing constraints to women's participation in the labor market can promote this kind of outcome and accelerate the pace of poverty reduction in Uganda.

Source: Canagarajah, Newman, and Bhattamishra (2001).

---

of entrepreneurial activity. The definition of entrepreneurship includes self-employment in any kind of remunerated activity and includes the informal sector. The figure compares with a TEA index of 12.0 in the United States and 1.6 in France. The study points out that the relationship between entrepreneurship and growth is complex, as in Uganda especially the question of how entrepreneurship translates into economic development and poverty reduction remains open.[2] In developing countries, women are more likely to prefer wage employment over entrepreneurship if available, but necessity often dictates that they start their own businesses. In Uganda it is not uncommon for people to engage in some kind of business activities in addition to wage employment or to run several small business ventures at once. The Global Entrepreneurship Monitor study points to the existence of marked regional differences in entrepreneurship, with the Eastern districts showing "spectacularly high" rates of entrepreneurial activity but poverty rates that have risen sharply in recent years. Unfortunately, the data were not disaggregated by gender and subjected to gender analysis. Doing so could yield interesting insights given the study's national coverage and large sample size.

The different structural roles of men and women in the economy (notably in agriculture and the informal sector) are coupled with their equally different—and unbalanced—roles in the household economy (figure 2.1 and box 2.1). Throughout Sub-Saharan Africa the boundary between economic and household activity is more fluid than in other regions. In addition to their prominence in agriculture, women bear the brunt of domestic tasks: processing food crops, providing water and firewood, caring for the elderly and the sick. This "double workday" contributes markedly to women's

Figure 2.1. Allocation of Time by Men and Women in Katebe, Rakai

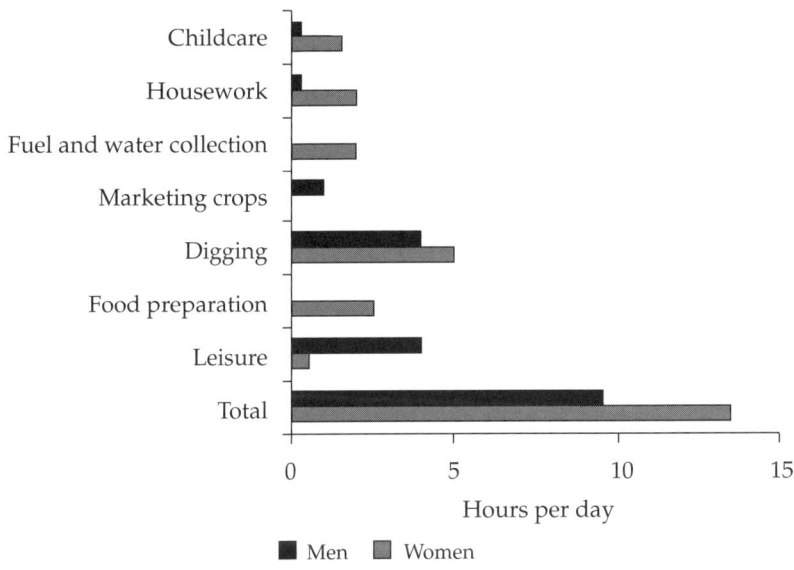

Hours per day

■ Men ■ Women

Source: UPPAP (2002).

Box 2.2. Analyzing Time Allocation by Men and Women in Uganda Is Critical

Analyzing time allocation by men and women is critical, for three key reasons. First, time allocation data in Uganda, as elsewhere in Sub-Saharan Africa, reveal not only the substantial market economy contributions of men and women to Uganda's development but also, and just as important, the existence of a whole realm of human activity—the household economy. This economy, in which most women work, is largely invisible and uncounted. Second, once the coexistence and interdependence of these economies become apparent, cross-sectoral and cross-task synergies and tradeoffs assume particular importance in identifying constraints to raising growth and productivity and in setting policy and program priorities. Third, time constraints were a critical (if insufficiently appreciated) issue before the HIV/AIDS pandemic. The advent of HIV/AIDS has exacerbated the time constraints across the two economies and given added urgency to addressing them as a matter of priority in poverty reduction strategies.

"overburden," as shown in the Uganda Participatory Poverty Assessment Process/Participatory Poverty Assessment 2 analysis. That analysis forcefully brought to light the problem of women's overburden and identified the strong imbalance in the gender division of labor as one of the major contributors to poverty. Women work substantially more than men, in both the market and the household economies. On average their workday may be 50 percent longer, and their work is closely integrated with household production systems.

Time constraints affect women disproportionately and mean that women have to trade off among necessary or important tasks, including developing or expanding their own businesses. Women have to undertake business activities in ways that are compatible with meeting their domestic responsibilities. Consequently, business registration or gaining access to banks and other financial institutions that involves travel, waiting, or delays constitutes an especially heavy burden for women.

Education and Fertility

Uganda has made impressive progress in education. As a result of universal primary education, primary enrollment rose from 3.0 million in 1997 to 7.6 million in 2003, with the percentage of girls rising steadily to 49.3 percent in 2003. Despite these significant achievements, however, the lowest income quintiles are less likely to attend primary school than higher income quintiles or to do so consistently. At the secondary level, the majority of the population has limited access, and gender inequalities remain large, with 20–35 percent more boys in S1–S4 and more than 60 percent more boys in S5–S6.[3]

The well-established link between education and fertility is confirmed in Uganda (figure 2.2). The total fertility rate is 7.8 among women with no education and 7.3 among women with some primary education (Uganda Bureau of Statistics 2000). Among women with more than primary education, the total fertility rate dropped from about 5.0 in 1988 to 3.9 in 2000. This means that on average, women with no education have about four children more than women with some secondary education. Gender inequality in education, employment, earnings, and bargaining power within families play significant roles in keeping Uganda's fertility rates among the highest in the world.

Inequality of access to education and training retards economic growth. A study of more than 100 countries over three decades finds that an increase of 1 percentage point in the share of adult women with secondary education implies an increase in per capita income growth of up to 0.3 percentage points (Dollar and Gatti 1999).

Figure 2.2. Fertility Trends by Level of Women's Education, 1988–2000

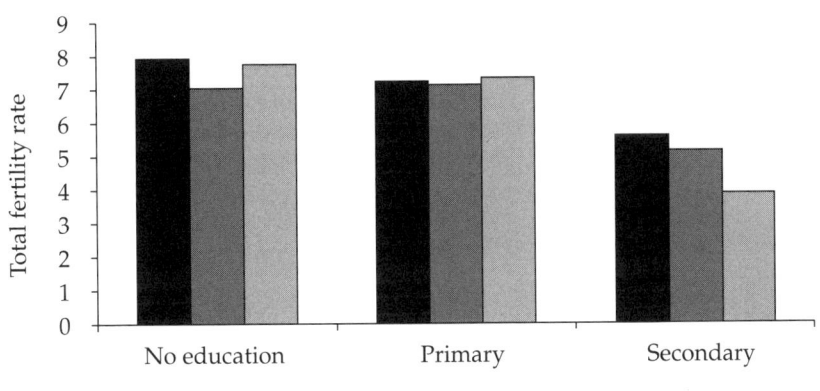

Does Gender Inequality Limit Growth in Uganda?

A growing body of microeconomic evidence and case study material suggests ways in which gender inequality affects growth, output, and productivity, especially in agriculture (box 2.3). Poor farmers are unwilling to diversify into nontraditional agricultural exports because of lack of sufficient labor (household and hired) (Kasente and others 2002; see Keller 2003 for a wider review of these issues). But women are particularly labor constrained, and they are more committed than men to using labor for food crop production to ensure household food security.

When asked about their problems in expanding agricultural production, men identified transport and marketing difficulties and lack of access to credit, problems that are already being targeted by government initiatives. Women, in contrast, identified problems related to agricultural production per se, in particular their labor constraints. When asked about the causes of labor constraints, men said simply that they had no money to hire labor. Women cited the time they spent looking after their families, working on their husbands' gardens and producing food for their households as reasons for inability to expand their production for the market.

Men and women face entirely different incentives as economic producers, incentives that depend on who controls the resulting income (box 2.4). When asked about their crop preferences as part of the Uganda Participatory Poverty Assessment Process/Participatory Poverty Assessment 2 exercise,

---

Box 2.3. Gender and Growth: Missed Potential

Studies in a variety of Sub-Saharan countries reveal the missed potential for increasing growth by addressing gender issues. In Burkina Faso shifting existing resources between men's and women's plots within the same household could increase output 10–20 percent. In Kenya giving women farmers the same level of agricultural inputs and education as men could increase yields obtained by women by more than 20 percent. In Tanzania reducing time burdens of women could increase household cash incomes for smallholder coffee and banana growers by 10 percent, labor productivity by 15 percent, and capital productivity by 44 percent. In Zambia if women enjoyed the same overall degree of capital investment in agricultural inputs, including land, as their male counterparts, total output could increase by as much as 15 percent.

Source: Blackden and Bhanu (1999).

Box 2.4. Incentives Affect Women's Responses to Uganda's Strategic Exports Initiative

Gender inequality affects the implementation of Uganda's Strategic Exports Initiative (Booth and others 2003, cited in World Bank 2005b). The Poverty and Social Impact Assessment of the Strategic Exports Initiative notes that the supply response sought under the strategy was limited by gender inequality, as the strategy failed to recognize that one of the principal determinants of response is the way incentives are mediated, at the household and community level, by negotiated relationships of cooperation and by conflict between men and women. Differing incentives in turn affect household income and how it is distributed. The Poverty and Social Impact Assessment points out that both incentive and intrahousehold distributional issues center on the monopolization of major income streams by men.

---

women listed cassava, beans, sweet potatoes, and plantains, because they contribute to household food security (sweet potatoes can also be sold). In contrast, men cited coffee and vanilla, 90 percent of the income from which they control (Keller 2003).

The Uganda Participatory Poverty Assessment Process/Participatory Poverty Assessment 2 draws attention to a widely known phenomenon in

Uganda and elsewhere in the subregion: when there is a market for a food crop that was previously grown for household consumption, control over disposal of that crop passes from women's to men's hands. The assessment draws an important policy conclusion from this: the decrease in poverty that is expected to follow from a shift to market-oriented production may disproportionately favor men (UPPAP 2002).

The focus of female activity on noncash crops and microenterprises means that women's formal contribution to economic growth in Uganda is limited. But women clearly have the potential to contribute more—as entrepreneurs, employers, and employees—enhancing domestic investment rates and participating as suppliers to foreign investors. In the microfinance context, women in Uganda are highly creditworthy, with excellent repayment rates (interview with Pride Uganda, November 2004).

Removing constraints on women's labor will be a critical factor in modernizing agricultural production in Uganda. Several studies have documented that women withhold their labor from the household production of cash crops because they know they will not benefit from the income earned (Muhereza 2001). If such a scenario is common, as is suspected, it will limit the opportunities to shift subsistence-oriented households toward market-oriented production, hindering initiatives to improve their well-being. These differences have broad implications for Uganda's growth prospects, particularly for implementation of the Program for the Modernization of Agriculture and revision and updating of the Uganda Public-Private Partnership.

Gender and Growth: A Macro Perspective

Extensive microeconomic analysis reveals the ways in which gender inequality limits productivity, output, and growth, especially in agriculture. Case study analysis suggests that gender differences in access to assets limit women's options, that gender differences in labor remuneration lead to conflict and affect labor allocation at the household level, and that gender differences in labor (and other factor) productivity limit economic efficiency and output. Macroeconomic analysis of the determinants of growth that use gender-focused variables has yielded similar results (box 2.5).

The 2004 Poverty Eradication Action Plan makes a similar argument and includes a higher estimate of diminished national output resulting from gender differences in economic incentives.

It notes that women do not always share in the benefits of production, even when they have done most of the work. According to the report, women in the early 1990s were much less enthusiastic than men about tobacco because men control the resulting income. A study of West Africa calculates that the gender-based disincentive effect reduced output there

---

Box 2.5. How Do Gender Differences in Education and Employment Affect Growth?

Cross-country growth regressions in Sub-Saharan Africa reveal the impact of gender differences in education and employment on growth. Between 1960 and 1992, the limited education and employment opportunities for women in Sub-Saharan Africa reduced annual per capita growth by 0.8 percentage points. This is significant, as a boost of 0.8 percentage points a year would have doubled economic growth over the past 30 years. The analysis suggests that gender inequality appears to account for about 15–20 percent of the difference in growth performance between Sub-Saharan Africa and East Asia. The size of these effects is considerable and gives credence to the argument that one important element in Africa's low growth may be the high level of gender inequality in education and employment. While gender inequality is not the main cause of poverty in Sub-Saharan Africa, it is an important element in accounting for the region's poor economic performance.

Although growth regressions must be interpreted with caution, these results are striking and suggest that economic growth in Sub-Saharan Africa could increase significantly if gender-based obstacles to growth were eliminated, a point made forcefully in *Can Africa Claim the 21st Century?* (Gelb 2000). Applying these aggregate model results to Uganda suggests that Uganda could gain up to 2 percentage points of GDP growth a year by addressing structural gender-based inequalities in education (total years of schooling) and formal sector employment.

Source: Klasen (*1988*), cited in Blackden and Bhanu (1999).

---

by 10–15 percent (Udry and others 1995). If the size of the effects in Uganda is similar, the Poverty Eradication Action Plan estimates the benefit of changing these incentives could amount to a one-time increase of about 5 percent of GDP. Gender-based capacity and incentive differences are therefore likely to have a significant impact on implementation of the Program for Modernization of Agriculture.

Conclusions

Because gender inequality acts as a powerful constraint to growth, removing gender-based barriers would make a substantial contribution to helping Uganda realize its growth potential and achieve the growth targets articulated in the Poverty Eradication Action Plan.

Macro analysis, case studies, and analysis of demographic linkages, asset inequality, and labor constraints all indicate that there is a strong connection between gender inequality and growth. Consequently, it is critical that growth-enhancing and poverty-reducing policies take account of these gender-based influences on, and obstacles to, growth. Policies must tackle these gender inequalities not only to promote equity and justice but also to promote economic growth and efficiency. The leadership exercised by the Government of Uganda, notably by the Ministry of Finance, Planning and Economic Development, in beginning to address the linkages between gender and growth in economic policymaking through the ongoing Poverty Reduction Support Credit process is very encouraging. It will be important to address these linkages explicitly, both through the wider articulation of the country's pro-poor growth strategy and as the government moves forward in its efforts to strengthen the Uganda Public-Private Partnership. This is especially important in the context of promoting the private sector and developing women's entrepreneurship.

Notes

1. This chapter draws on the World Bank's Strategic Country Gender Assessment (World Bank 2005b) and on consultations with women entrepreneurs in Uganda.

2. The study distinguishes between "necessity" and "opportunity" entrepreneurship. "Necessity" entrepreneurship is seen as involuntary and motivated by necessity, while "opportunity" entrepreneurship is voluntary and motivated by the pursuit of perceived opportunities. Both types of entrepreneurship exist at high levels in Uganda.

3. Uganda's education system is based on the British system. S1–S6 are levels of secondary education.

3

Establishing a Business: Registration, Approvals, and Access to Finance and Capital

Ensuring a good environment for the start-up and expansion of women-owned businesses, helping women to overcome barriers to business creation and development are important for national economic growth.

—OECD (2001)

Uganda: Administrative Barriers to Investment Update (FIAS 2003) identifies a number of barriers to business entry in Uganda, for both foreign investors and local investors seeking to enter the formal sector. These barriers relate to the formation and registration of companies, the registration of business names, registration with the Uganda Investment Authority to obtain an investment license, acquisition of trade licenses (under the Trade License Act) from the relevant local council or authority, and immigration procedures. Key recommendations included computerizing, simplifying forms, combining business registration and taxpayer identification numbers, eliminating the investment license, streamlining trade license reform efforts, and streamlining the procedure for obtaining a work permit.

This assessment endorses those recommendations, which are designed to affect all businesses in Uganda. In addition, it considers issues specifically affecting business start-ups by women—aspects of the registration and licensing formalities and issues relating to access to finance for business purposes.

Registration and Licensing Procedures Are Cumbersome and Costly

There are various stages along the road to establishing a "formal" business in Uganda. An enterprise must have fixed premises, obtain a trade license, pay local taxes, register a business name, incorporate as a company, and pay taxes to the Uganda Revenue Authority. Formalizing a business is important, because formalization is frequently seen as a critical step to business growth. Company formation in particular is seen as important, both because the limited liability status of companies encourages risk-taking and because the share structure facilitates the pooling of resources (Gower, Prentice, and Pettet 1979; Economist 1999).

About 90 percent of businesses in Uganda are sole proprietorships. Women own 39 percent of the businesses in the Uganda Business Register (Government of Uganda 2002b). This figure understates their role as business owners, because the register includes only businesses with fixed premises. Many women operate their micro or small-scale businesses without this degree of formalization. The challenge is to legitimize and strengthen the base of their activity, so that they can expand their enterprises.

Businesses in Uganda are required either to incorporate as companies with their own separate legal identity under the Companies Act or to register their business name under the Business Names Registration Act.[1] In addition, when they begin trading, all businesses are required to obtain a trade license from the Local Council, under the Trade Licensing Act. Problems have arisen from the lack of transparency in the system and from the use of trade licenses to enforce a separate taxation system (graduated tax) (box 3.1).

While the delays and costs of registration and licensing processes impose a burden on all businesses, evidence from the Government of Uganda's Regulatory Best Practice Program suggests that such requirements impose a disproportionate burden on enterprises headed by women (box 3.2):

- Women perceive the regulatory burden to be greater than men.
- Enterprises headed by women are much more likely to be subject to harassment, including requests to pay bribes and threats of closure; women are seen as "soft targets." Women are time poor, with greater family and domestic responsibilities than men. As a result, they are less inclined to register and formalize their businesses when procedures are complex and time consuming.

Women entrepreneurs respond well to simplifications in the system and will come into compliance if it becomes feasible for them to do so.

The emerging evidence suggests that while for enterprises owned by men registration and licensing procedures may add to the cost of formalizing a business, for micro- and small-scale women entrepreneurs, they may represent an absolute barrier that can prevent them from formalizing their business. The difference may reflect women's domestic duties, the time required to register a business, and the fact that as women do not con-

Box 3.1. Trade Licensing Creates Particular Problems for Women in Uganda

A woman bar owner in Uganda describes the problems that trade licensing created for her:

> I am a bar owner. When I was starting up my business four years ago, I went to the licensing authorities to inquire on the procedure. I was given the application forms at a cost of Ush 2,500, which I filled in. On returning them the following day, I was given two inspectors to verify the information presented. These inspectors were the health inspector and a council officer. We went to my business premises and looked around for about 25 minutes. After the inspections, we went back to the council offices and I was issued an invoice for a trade licenses fee. I paid for the fee, but they refused to give me the trade license, insisting that I present my graduated tax ticket. I had no money, so I had to take time off from my business to go to a friend and borrow money so that I could pay my graduated tax to receive my trading license.
>
> Last year I was issued a trading license without the presentation of the graduated tax ticket. Two weeks later, when the council officials were making enforcement visits, they came to my premises and asked for both the graduated tax and trading license. Unfortunately, I had only the trading license. They closed my business and would reopen it only if I paid my graduated tax. I had to bribe them the following day with Ush 5,000 to reopen. After a few days I was able to pay my graduated tax.
>
> The authorities should be consistent in their requirements, rules, and procedures, and separate other taxes from business licenses, levies, and taxes. Graduated taxes should not have a bearing on the operations of the business.

Source: Kirkpatrick and Lawson (2004).

trol the cash in the household, the fees (legitimate or illegitimate) may impose an insurmountable burden.

The government is taking steps to streamline the registration and licensing burden on businesses. The Uganda Law Reform Commission recently produced a draft Companies Bill, which would go some way toward improving the situation. The bill would permit companies with a single shareholder to be formalized (under the current law, companies must have at least two shareholders). The change would mean that a woman would no longer have

Box 3.2. The Effect of Regulatory Reform on Female-Headed Enterprises in Uganda: Emerging Evidence

The *Uganda Regulatory Cost Survey Report 2004*, covering 241 enterprises in 4 regions, measured the compliance cost of registration and licensing requirements (Kirkpatrick and Lawson 2004). Its findings include the following:

- More than a quarter of all enterprises surveyed reported that government officials had "interfered" with their business—by threatening to close it or asking for bribes, for example. Among enterprises headed by women, the figure was 43 percent.
- Forty percent of microenterprises headed by women felt that the total burden of regulation was "heavy" or "severe"; for businesses headed by men, the figure was 35 percent.

Enterprises that Responded Government Officials Have "Interfered" with Their Businesses

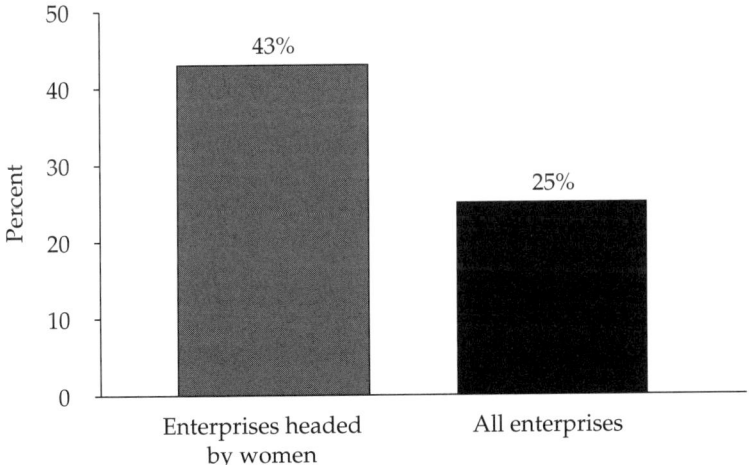

Source: Kirkpatrick and Lawson (2004).

Trade licenses were identified as the most burdensome regulation. A little more than 30 percent of men and more than 40 percent of women cited trade license procedures as an obstacle to the growth of their business.

(continued on the following page)

Box 3.2. (*continued*)

Enterprises that Responded Trade License Procedures Are Obstacles to Their Business Growth

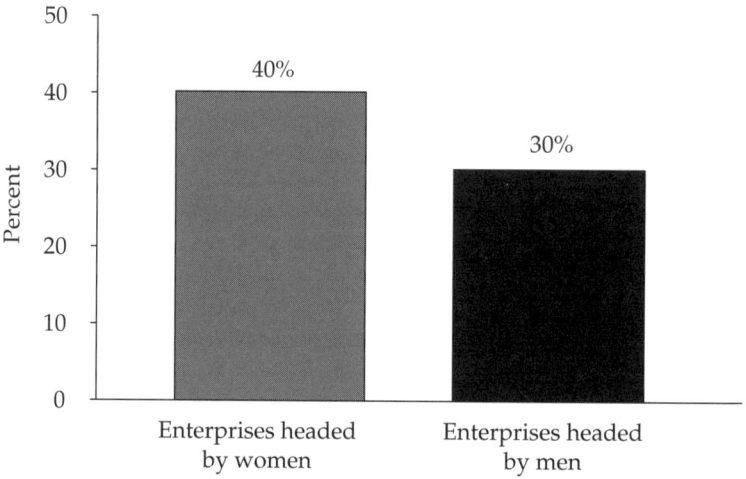

Source: Kirkpatrick and Lawson (2004).

The Regulatory Best Practice Program has started pilot projects to reduce the time and monetary cost of obtaining trade licenses by streamlining licensing procedures and reducing the number of approvals. A pilot project in Entebbe Municipality reduced the time spent by Ugandan businesses in obtaining licenses by 90 percent, reduced compliance costs by 75 percent, and increased revenue collection by 40 percent. The Impact Assessment of the first pilot (which has recently won an International Investors award) suggests that the reforms have encouraged women to obtain licenses: most of the license applications from women were first-time registrations.

Source: UMACIS (2003).

to find a co-shareholder (frequently her husband, who is thus given a formal stake in her company). The bill would also potentially simplify the forms to be completed in order register a business (the exact effects of this will become clearer once regulations under the act are produced).

The Trade Licensing Act provides for local governments to issue trade licenses based on a schedule of fees determined by the location and type of business.[2] Many businesses regard these licenses as the most onerous of the regulatory requirements. Initiatives are being taken under the Regulatory Best Practice Program, under the Local Government Reform Program, and by the Uganda Law Reform Commission to simplify trade licensing procedures. Pilot projects that have focused on simplifying administrative procedures, particularly those described in box 3.2, have reduced the administrative burden on businesses and had a particularly positive impact on businesses headed by women. Concern has been expressed, however, that with the planned abolition of the graduated tax, local governments will look to trade licenses as a source of alternative funding.

International benchmarking with other countries that originally had legal frameworks similar to Uganda's shows that countries that have undertaken fundamental reform of their business start-up requirements (Australia, Canada, and New Zealand) have reduced the cost and time of compliance (table 3.1).

The 2004 Regulatory Cost Survey Report (Kirkpatrick and Lawson 2004) suggests that trade licenses are the most burdensome regulation for women entrepreneurs; owners of small-scale microenterprises do not try to regis-

Table 3.1. Costs of Registering a Business in Selected Commonwealth Countries

Country	Cost (% GNI per capita)	Duration (days)	Number of procedures
New Zealand	0.2	12	2
Canada	1.0	3	2
Australia	2.1	2	2
Hong Kong, China	3.4	11	5
Botswana	11.3	108	11
Kenya	53.4	47	12
Uganda	**131.3**	**36**	**17**
Tanzania	186.9	35	13

Source: http://rru.worldbank.org/DoingBusiness/ExploreTopics/StartingBusiness/Compare All.aspx?direction=asc.

Note: Data from the World Bank's Doing Business data base (http://rru.worldbank.org/ DoingBusiness/) are derived from surveys of 130 economies. The survey examines commercial or industrial firms with up to 50 employees and start-up capital of 10 times the economy's per capita Gross National Income. Information is gathered from the country's largest city only. The survey counts all procedures (defined as a legal requirement that involves a separate interaction between the firm and an outside entity) required to register a firm. Data also include screening procedures by a set of overseeing government entities, tax- and labor-related registration procedures, health and safety procedures, and environment-related procedures.

ter their companies. It is nevertheless important that a streamlined and appropriate legislative and administrative framework be put in place for company formation if the vision of the Poverty Eradication Action Plan of transforming Uganda into a middle-income industrial country is to be realized. Company registration is seen as key to business growth, encouraging risk-taking and the pooling of resources. The onerous and extremely costly regime, combined with the complex legal requirements for forming a company under the current Companies Act (and even under the Uganda Law Reform Commission's proposals for reform) makes registering a company impossible for many women entrepreneurs.

In view of the barriers that current regulation and licensing requirements are imposing on business as a whole and on women entrepreneurs in particular, urgent consideration should be given to a much more fundamental approach to deregulating registration and licensing requirements than has been undertaken. Key reforms in best practice Commonwealth countries that previously had a Companies Act (based on the 1948 Companies Act of England and Wales) and business name registration regime similar to Uganda's current one include the following:

- Australia, Canada, and New Zealand abolished the requirement that companies have memoranda and articles. Registration in these countries is done through a simple form.
- Australia, Canada, England and Wales, and New Zealand abolished the need to involve lawyers in forming a company by simplifying registration procedures.[3]
- England and Wales and Hong Kong (China) abolished registration of business names for unincorporated businesses.[4] In Uganda this would mean repealing the Business Names Registration Act.

International experience suggests that these type of reforms result in gains. In Uganda such reforms could have a disproportionate effect on the ability of women to register and legitimize their businesses. To achieve these results, the government could take several steps:

- Adopt reforms of the Companies Act and the Business Names Registration Act that have been successful in high-performing Commonwealth countries. These include incorporating a company by way of a simple form rather than by filing memoranda and articles, abolishing the requirement to use a lawyer to form a company (section 67 of the Advocates Act), and abolishing the system of business name registration for unincorporated businesses.
- In view of the negative impact that trade licensing has on all enterprises, especially businesses headed by women, go beyond current pilot pro-

jects, which focus on administrative reform of the existing system. Undertake more fundamental reform of both the Trade Licensing Act and the Local Government Act, which gives local governments wide powers to impose taxes, fees, permits, rents, and licenses. Principles and examples of regulatory best practice are given in *Uganda: Administrative Barriers to Investment Update* (FIAS 2003).

- Reform the registration and licensing process in order to reduce barriers that prevent women from registering their businesses or obtaining licenses. Examples include expanding opening hours and changing staff attitudes.

Women Lack Adequate Access to Finance

Uganda has much less private credit (6 percent of GDP) than the median country in Sub-Saharan Africa (12 percent). Because of its large fiscal deficit, real lending rates remain very high (1,000 percent in the past six years), constraining private sector development (Government of Uganda 2004c).

Women entrepreneurs face a clear gender bias in access to credit, receiving just 9 percent of available credit (about 1 percent in rural areas) (Mukasa and others 2004; Tripp and Kwesiga 2002). Women do have access to informal saving mechanisms and to microfinance, especially group lending, through about 1,500 microfinance operations in Uganda (consultations with the Directorate for Economic Affairs, Ministry of Finance, Planning and Economic Development, November 2004). Some, including the Uganda Women's Finance Trust, which is currently in the process of restructuring, cater to women. This form of financing has its limitations, however, particularly for women who wish to grow their enterprises. The high interest rates, small loans sizes, and short-term nature of the loans mean that women can become trapped in the informal sector and unable to expand their businesses.

A product designed to address the demand for longer term financing for purchase of capital items is the capital assets loan (Kikalu) (box 3.3). The loan is based on the group lending model.

There are some signs that women's access to finance is slowly improving. The Microfinance Deposits Institutions Act of 2003 may enable the sector to operate a more viable business service, especially through the new ability to take savings. Some mainstream financial institutions are expressing an interest in financing small and medium-size enterprises. For the time being, however, the "missing middle" in business financing—and the consequent limited access to capital—remains an obstacle for many women entrepreneurs.

A number of factors explain the difficulties women face when seeking finance for their businesses. These include the following:

- Traditional financial institutions engage in gender bias. One professional woman was told that she could not open a personal bank account with-

---

Box 3.3 Uganda's Capital Asset (Kikalu) Loan

In 1999 the Council for the Economic Empowerment of Women in Africa-Uganda (CEEWA-U) surveyed 325 clients from 27 microfinance institutions in Uganda and conducted a Participatory Rural Appraisal with clients from three microfinance institutions. The study revealed that microfinance institution clients needed and wanted longer repayment periods and larger loans to purchase fixed or current assets. Clients also indicated that they borrow from several institutions at the same time. Since they cannot admit to having multiple loans, they do not reveal the information, increasing the risk to microfinance institutions.

Based on this information, CEEWA-U and the Uganda Microfinance Union designed a new loan product—the capital asset loan, popularly known as Kikalu—to address these clients' needs. The Kikalu is a combination of a capital asset loan and a working capital loan. The capital asset loan has a 6- to 12-month repayment period, while the working capital loan has the usual 16-week cycle. The requirements for taking out the loan (which is unsecured) are as follows:

- The borrower must be an established client of a microfinance institution.
- The borrower must have an ongoing business
- The borrower must have borrowed at least three times and repaid without missing a scheduled payment.
- The borrower may opt to have a regular capital working loan from the microfinance institution and take out only the capital asset loan.
- The loan is extended only to business sectors (commerce, the service sector, agriculture, manufacturing, housing).
- The minimum loan size is Ush 300,000.
- Repayment is on a monthly basis for 6–12 months.
- The references on the membership form guarantee the loan. All core group members guarantee the loan.
- The interest rate is based on the microfinance institution's cost.

---

out her husband's co-signature, despite the fact that the law does not require such a signature.

- The very common requirement for land as collateral operates as an absolute block to many enterprises headed by women, because land is not readily accessible to women, due to land allocation practices that favor men.
- Financial institutions in Uganda accept assets such as book debts, merchandise, stock, and machinery as collateral. But Uganda's unclear and outdated moveable personal property security laws mean that such

forms of financing are readily available only in the form of fixed and floating charges over the assets of businesses that have incorporated under the Companies Act. Businesses that are not registered as companies are constrained from using nonland assets as collateral.

- Formal credit information is lacking. Microfinance institutions perceive women as sound risks, with high repayment rates. But lack of credit information means that it is difficult for women to benefit from their good records. There is no credit reference bureau in Uganda, and information on judgment debtors is not readily available from the courts. A dysfunctional companies registry means that even basic and legally required financial information about formal businesses registered as companies is not available from annual returns.
- Women have limited knowledge about the information required to obtain finance from formal institutions. Most women have weak formal business skills and lack audited accounts.

A number of approaches can be taken to address women's limited access to business finance. These include working with commercial banks to design products and services that are more appropriate for women customers, building capacity among women entrepreneurs to enhance their ability to apply for finance, and adopting legal and administrative reforms. There is clearly a need to enhance the ability of women to access land, a prerequisite for collateral for much lending in Uganda. (This complex issue is addressed in chapter 4.) There is also a need to enhance the ability of women to use nonland assets (such as stock or machinery) as collateral. A first step would be to put in place a coherent legal framework for moveable personal property. The useful mechanism of a floating charge over nonland assets is currently not available to unincorporated businesses in Uganda, and other forms of financing that use moveable personal property as security, such as debt factoring and retention of title clauses, are virtually unknown. The Chattels Transfer Act, which provides the legal framework for some types of nonland security, is rarely used, and the register of chattels mortgages it provides for is nonexistent.

Recognizing the importance of reform in this area, the Uganda Law Reform Commission produced a Chattels Securities Bill in 2004. This bill lays the foundation for a comprehensive and coherent system for recognizing and ranking security interests in moveable personal property, including the establishment of a register in which such interests may be entered to secure their priority. The bill is based on established international best practice for moveable personal property security regimes (Article 9 of the U.S. Uniform Commercial Code, which has been recommended or adopted in various common law jurisdictions).[5] The excellent regime that would be established by the bill is to a large degree undermined by the proposal to retain the provisions on creating and registering debentures in the draft Companies Bill. It is strongly recommended that the Uganda Law Reform Commission revisit this proposal, which would result in two concurrent regimes and a dual registration system, largely defeating the purpose of the proposed Chattels Securities Act, which is to provide a comprehensive and transparent system for recognizing and ranking nonland security interests.

The final recommendation for the Government of Uganda to take forward is to promote systems that enable women to benefit from the good credit records they have established. It is hoped that the initiative by the Association of Micro Finance Institutions of Uganda (AMFIU) to build a management information system to allow all members to store data, including gender-disaggregated data, will provide a basis for women entrepreneurs, to "graduate" from microfinance, as data are shared with commercial banks. In addition, it is recommended that the government make publicly available data it already has on bad debtors through the court system. A credit registry is needed. It is recommended that the judiciary establish a publicly accessible register of judgment debts, ideally encompassing Local Council and Magistrates Courts. This would enable basic information about defaulters to be accessed by potential lenders.

There is scope for NGOs in Uganda to build on the success of the Kikalu initiative and take further action to address women's limited access to finance. Possible actions include the following:

- Increase awareness of women-friendly sources of capital (such as the Kikalu loan).
- Work with commercial banks to raise awareness of market opportunity (as the Uganda Women Entrepreneurs Association Limited has done with Barclays).
- Enhance the provision of business development services and relevant technical training for women entrepreneurs.

Notes

1. Registration is also possible under the Co-operative Society Statute, but this form of registration is unusual. An exception to the requirement to register a business name is the case in which the name of the proprietor is used as the trading name.

2. The Trade Licensing Act applies only to trading businesses, not to service deliverers.

3. In Uganda lawyers have a virtual monopoly on company formation, charging a fee of 10 percent of the nominal capital on Ush 75,000–Ush 1 million. With some very limited exceptions, the Advocates Act makes it illegal for anyone other than an attorney to prepare any document for a fee "for or in relation to the formation of any limited company whether private or public."

4. In England and Wales, the Business Names Act 1985 controls the use of misleading business names by requiring that permission be obtained to use certain potentially misleading names. It does not impose a blanket registration requirement, as does the Ugandan law. In Hong Kong (China) businesses are required to register with the tax authority.

5. Article 9 of the U.S. Uniform Commercial Code has been in force for more than 20 years in nearly all the U.S. states. It is the foundation of several acts passed in a number of provinces in Canada, including Alberta, Manitoba, Ontario, Saskatchewan, and Yukon Territory. The European Bank for Reconstruction and Development has produced a Model Law on Secured Transactions (EBRD 1994), which is based on similar principles, as is New Zealand's new Personal Property Securities Act.

4

Locating a Business: Access to Land and Site Development

Women of Africa toil all their lives on land that they do not own, to produce what they do not control, and at the end of their marriage, through divorce or death, they can be sent away empty handed.

—President Julius Nyerere,
Third World Conference on Women, 1984

The *Uganda: Administrative Barriers to Investment Update* (FIAS 2003) makes recommendations about access to land, planning policies, site development, and utilities and environmental issues. This chapter examines the gender dimension of some of these issues, considering in particular issues relating to land and private sector development in Uganda.

Land is of central importance to Uganda's growth agenda, not least because of the importance of agriculture to the economy and the dominant role of women in agriculture. Agriculture remains central to Uganda's economy, and land is the major productive asset. More than 40 percent of GDP and 85 percent of export earnings come from the agricultural sector, made up mainly of smallholder farms that depend on family labor. Women provide 70 percent of agricultural labor and 60 percent of the labor used to raise cash crops, such as coffee, cotton, and tea (Uganda Land Alliance 2000, cited in Asiimwe 2002). Despite this, households headed by women are significantly less likely to report cultivable land among their assets or to have access to or control of land. Women hold only 7 percent of registered land titles in Uganda (Government of Uganda 1999).

Women's limited ability to own land and their insecure rights to occupy it affect their ability to invest and contribute to Uganda's economic growth. Because of their lack of security of tenure and lack of control over economic activities, they have limited incentive to develop the land they occupy. Women's lack of land title, required for collateral for business loans, means that they have limited access to finance. In addition, they have limited access to land to locate business premises, particularly in areas of customary land (the situation may be better in urban areas).

Why Do So Few Women in Uganda Have Control over Land?

Ugandan women have little control over land, for a variety of reasons.

Cultural Norms Limit Women's Right to Inherit Land

Women are denied opportunities to inherit land due to cultural norms—systems of patrilineal inheritance and patrilocal residence. When a man dies, his heir is determined by the cultural leaders of his clan. Because heritage is patrilineal, it is customary for land to pass to the man's relatives, his wife becoming heir in only a few instances (Government of Uganda 2001). Under customary law, widows are to be taken care of by their husband's relatives (including through the practice of widow inheritance, the inheritance of the widow and her children by the brother of the deceased husband), but in practice it is common for a widow to be thrown off the land, with no provision made for her welfare. Anecdotal evidence suggests that HIV/AIDS has made this occurrence more frequent, with relatives telling AIDS widows and their children that as they are unlikely to have long to live, there is no point in them staying on the land.

The formal legal position is rather different. The Constitution provides for the protection of the rights of widows and widowers to inherit property of their deceased spouses. The Succession Act specifies that when a husband dies without leaving a will, his widow or widows receive 15 percent of the matrimonial property. The Succession (Amendment) Bill prepared by the Uganda Law Reform Commission has the stated aim of amending the Succession Act to bring it into line with the provisions on equality of sexes in matters of succession as enshrined in the Constitution. It would entitle the spouse to one half of the matrimonial home and household chattels (with all wives sharing equally), with the other half distributed equally among the children of the deceased.

Divorce Rules Limit Women's Control over Land

Upon divorce it is difficult for a woman to assert her rights over matrimonial land, as under customary law she has no rights to it. Even under formal law, when a wife seeks to claim a stake in marital property not directly acquired during the marriage, she is deemed to lack legal and equitable rights in it and her contribution to the home during the marriage is usually not taken into account when the assets are divided between the divorcing spouses (Banenya 2002).

Limited Access to Justice Inhibits Women's Ability to Assert Their Rights

Even where the law protects their right to land, women are often unaware that such protection exists or unable to assert their legal rights. A Ugandan woman can assert her rights to assets on the death of her husband under the Succession Act through various paths (figure 4.1). The Uganda Law Reform Commission has proposed making justice more accessible by establishing a District Administrator General in every district.[1] The reality, however, is that the time, cost, and knowledge required to seek justice make the system inaccessible for many women.

As far as more general disputes over land are concerned, men bring four times as many cases to land tribunals than women (Mukasa and others 2004). Constraints that inhibit the ability of women to access these tribunals include inability to afford the fees, time poverty, and the perception that the tribunals are biased against women. Land matters are dealt with by Local Council 2 Courts in the first instance (figure 4.2). There is a requirement that women be represented on Local Council Courts, but the requirement is not always met (see chapter 7). A training manual has recently been drawn up for Local Council Courts that sets out guidelines on the princi-

Figure 4.1. Routes Available to a Ugandan Woman Deprived of Matrimonial Assets upon the Death of Her Husband

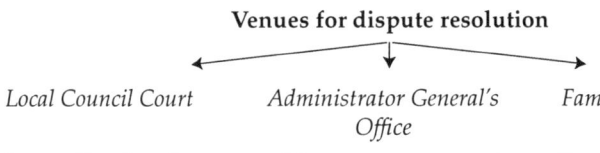

Venues for dispute resolution

Local Council Court	*Administrator General's Office*	*Family/clan meetings*
In practice, Local Council Courts tend to apply customary law, which upholds the rights of the husband's family to take the assets.	Many women cannot afford the cost and time of traveling to Kampala, where the Administrator General's Office is located.	Traditionally, women were not allowed to talk during family or clan meetings. Although this custom has changed, it remains hard for women, especially women with little education, to participate in these meetings.

Figure 4.2. Uganda's Land Dispute System

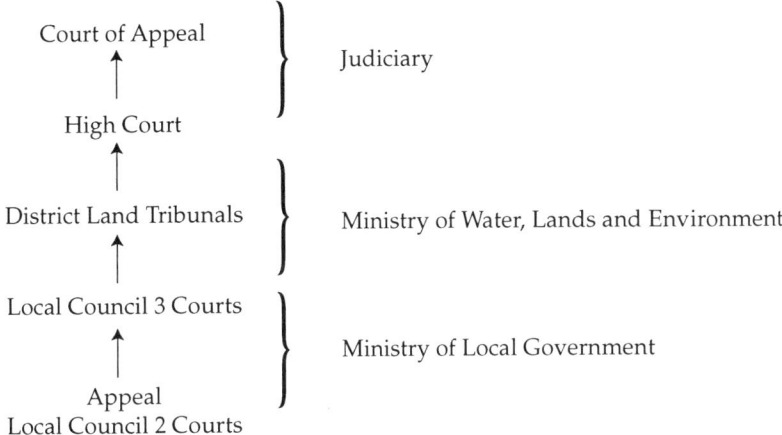

ples of equality of treatment, including the importance of not applying customs and cultural values against women and of not discriminating on the basis of marital status. Local Council Courts are supposed to receive training on the guidelines in 2005.

Registration of Land Title Is Limited

The Land Act 1998 provides for all land in Uganda to be registered.[2] The process of registration is an opportunity for women to assert their interest in land. However, only 25–30 percent of land in Uganda is currently registered, with only 15 percent of registrations described as "active" (the remainder are old registrations that no longer reflect the reality on the ground). The system of registration is costly and inaccessible (table 4.1). These issues are particularly acute for women, who have less time and less access to funds than men. Under the Land Sector Strategic Plan, the Ministry of Water, Lands and Environment intends to decentralize the system by establishing District Land Registries and registering customary land with subcounty chiefs and town clerks.

Where land registration has taken place, women are not commonly registered as owners, and their rights are not noted on the title. Of the applications for registration received by District Land Management Offices in 2000, only about 6 percent were from women (Government of Uganda 2003a) (figure 4.3).

Under the Systematic Demarcation Project (a pilot for first-time registration of customary land at the parish level), more than 95 percent of registrations were registered in the name of men (box 4.1).

Table 4.1. Cost of Registering Land in Selected Commonwealth Countries

Country	Time (days)	Cost (% of property per capita)
New Zealand	2	0.2
Canada	20	2.0
Kenya	39	4.0
Uganda	**48**	**5.5**
Tanzania	61	12.6
Botswana	69	5.0

Source: World Bank (2005b).

Figure 4.3. Land Registration Received by District Land Management Offices, 2000

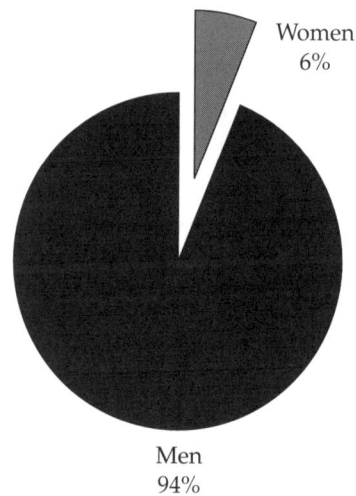

Women
6%

Men
94%

Source: Government of Uganda (2003b).

Land Issues Have a Significant Impact on Women's Ability to Contribute to Economic Growth

Women's lack of security of tenure and their low levels of participation and control over economic activities mean that choices about which crops to grow and how to use any income from their sale remain the preserve of men. Together with low levels of agricultural extension training for women farmers, this issue is central to Uganda's Strategic Exports Initiative.

Box 4.1. Uganda's Pilot Systematic Demarcation Project

The Ministry of Water, Land and Environment is piloting a Systematic Demarcation Project under the Land Sector Strategic Plan, with the aim of instituting a district level–led registration initiative. Registration takes place at the subcounty level, with the subcounty chief appointed registrar. The benefits of encouraging land registration are presented as providing title for collateral, minimizing land disputes, and enabling agricultural extension services to be more effective. So far, 3 (of more than 5,000) parishes—Ntungamo, Soroti, and Masaka—have participated in the project. Through a partnership between the Government of Uganda and NGOs, sensitization and training is taking place. Training on gender issues is a key element in the process.

The project has involved individualizing customary land and converting it to freehold. While men are willing to have their wives be noted on data collection sheets as spouses, registration of title in more than 95 percent of cases is in the sole name of the husband. Registration has taken place in the name of the wife in some cases in which the wife had bought the land herself or inherited it. In the first pilot, of several hundred registrations, only one married couple were prepared to register in joint names; they were better educated and had a larger plot than the rest of the population.

Source: Government of Uganda (2004b).

Reform Efforts

Gender issues remain a controversial theme as the Government of Uganda continues with the land reform process. The government is taking several steps to improve women's access to land.

The Land Act 1998 (as amended)

The key provision of the Land Act designed to enhance the security of occupancy of women is the provision that requires that disposition of family land (including by mortgage) take place only with the prior consent of the spouse. If such consent is not obtained, the transaction is void.

There are fundamental questions over the effectiveness of this provision. It is unclear how willing consent is when it is given—banks lending on the security of land report cases of forgery of signatures giving consent (and of certificates from Local Councils confirming the marital status of an applicant). From the point of view of Uganda's developing mortgage market, financial institutions are concerned at the increased costs of lending, and some have even stated that they will cease to take family land as security because of the uncertainties caused by the provision that the transaction is void if prior consent is not obtained.

Co-ownership: The Domestic Relations Bill

In its original form, the Land Act provided for co-ownership of matrimonial land. This clause disappeared during the Parliamentary process, however (Asiimwe 2002). Despite the efforts of women's groups to have this omission corrected, the co-ownership provision is not included in the legislation. The Domestic Relations Bill currently being considered by the Parliamentary Legal and Parliamentary Affairs Committee tackles the issues of land allocation and gender head on, by reinserting in the Land Act a provision giving a spouse automatic co-ownership rights. The provision is likely to be highly contentious, and it is far from clear that it will make the statute books. Tanzania is on the process of changing discriminatory regulations, in an effort that is an example of best practice (box 4.2).

Box 4.2. International Best Practice: Tanzania's Draft Land Mortgage Regulations

Tanzania's Land (Amendment) Act 2004 deals with the requirement to obtain the consent of a spouse for a mortgage of the matrimonial home. Regulations under the Act—the draft Land (Mortgage) Regulations—currently being considered by the Ministry of Land are designed to provide a balance between the rights of spouses and the rights of lenders. They set out the reasonable steps that a lender needs to take to ascertain the matrimonial status of an applicant. They also deal with the issue of ensuring that consent to the mortgage by a spouse is informed and genuine, providing a basic statutory minimum that if complied with will provide a good defense to any allegation that a lender should have taken more care before granting the mortgage. Steps to be taken by a lender include advising a spouse to obtain independent advice and obtaining written evidence that such advice has been obtained or that the spouse having been advised to take independent advice declined to do so.

Source: Law and Development Partnership, November 2004.

The Registration of Titles Act

The Land Sector Strategic Plan identifies harmonization of land legislation with the Constitution and the Land Act 1998 as a key priority. An important initiative in this respect is amendment of the Registration of Titles Act, which introduced the Torrens system of title by registration in Uganda.[3] The key principle of the Act is that the law recognizes the registrant(s) as the only rightful owner(s). Except in an unusual case (such as fraud), this means that the person registered as owner in the land register, has title to the land, and this cannot be successfully challenged.

Reform of the Act is being undertaken by the Ministry of Water, Land and Environment's Harmonization of Land Tenure Legislation Project (Government of Uganda 2004b).[4] The project has identified the issue of reconciling the Torrens approach with the rights created by the Land Act in favor of spouses (and other lawful and bona fide occupants). The reform of the Act is clearly an opportunity to enhance the ability of women to ensure that their rights appear on the register. Educating women about their legal rights is critical.

The Land Act Implementation: Land Sector Strategic Plan

The Land Sector Strategic Plan addresses the difficult issue of implementing the Land Act, in particular disseminating information about land rights and methods of asserting them. It recognizes the vulnerability of women in relation to security of tenure. Activities to address these issues include the following:

- development of checklists and guidelines for land sector activities in relation to the needs of both men and women in various vulnerable groups
- development of specific monitoring indicators for gender balance of programs
- undertaking of research, including research on barriers to women implementing the spousal consent provisions of the Land Act
- assessment of training needs to enable women to become more effective participants in land sector institutions
- addressing of gender issues in land information systems, including ensuring that data are disaggregated by gender.

Additional resources are needed to implement these activities effectively.

Recommendations

Promising efforts are underway to address the issues of women's access to land in Uganda. Building on these efforts, the government could pursue the following steps:

- Encourage the Systematic Demarcation Project to put additional emphasis on enabling women to assert their existing land rights. Registration as co-owners is proving culturally unacceptable in many cases. As an alternative, women could be encouraged to ensure that their right to consent to sale or mortgage of the matrimonial home is protected by way of a caveat on the register.
- In developing proposals for the reform of the Registration by Title Act, give priority to exploring new modes of registration that protect a spouse's interest in matrimonial land.
- Enact the provisions of the Domestic Relations Bill providing for co-ownership of matrimonial property. If the provisions cannot be enacted, as a fall back, explore the concept of giving a spouse a life interest in the matrimonial home. Such a life interest would protect the ability of the wife to stay in the matrimonial home during her lifetime while letting the land revert to her husband's clan on her death. The concept would thus not conflict with customary law provisions for widows. Such a proposal would affect both the Domestic Relations Bill and the Succession (Amendment) Bill.
- Amend the Succession Act to provide for equality of men and women in succession.
- Amend the provisions in the Domestic Relations Bill relating to the fair division of property on divorce.
- Develop regulations under the Land (Amendment) Act to specify the duty of lenders and purchasers in obtaining the consent of the spouse to dispositions of matrimonial land (see box 4.2). The regulations should provide for situations in which the spouse is illiterate and include measures to ensure that consent is freely given.
- Enhance the ability of women to access justice through the Administrator General's Department, the Local Council Courts, and the Land Tribunals (see chapter 7).

Notes

1. The bill is the Administrator General's Office (Amendment) (No.2) Bill.

2. Land in Uganda is classified as freehold, leasehold, customary, or *mailo* (registered land in Buganda). Land may be held in perpetuity, and the owners have the right to transfer title.

3. The system is modeled after the Land Transfer Act 1915 of the State of Victoria, Australia.

4. The Survey Act Cap 232 and the Land Acquisition Act Cap 226 are also to be amended under the project.

5

Operating a Business: Tax Administration and Customs

My aunt ended up going out of business because every time a tax inspector visited she paid whatever they asked in cash. She had no idea how to comply with the system.

—Ugandan woman lawyer

Uganda: Administrative Barriers to Investment Update (FIAS 2003) highlights a number of issues relating to tax and customs administration by the Uganda Revenue Authority (URA). These include the operation of value-added tax (VAT) refunds; the absence of clear URA guidelines, which has lead to contradictory interpretations of the income tax statute; legalistic operations of the Tax Appeal Tribunal; the absence of a risk-based system for customs inspections; the lack of transparency in customs valuations; a cumbersome duty drawback system; and corruption.

The FIAS report makes a number of recommendations regarding taxation administration and customs. These include introducing a single taxpayer number, reforming the VAT rebate system, simplifying tax appeal tribunal procedures, introducing risk-based customs inspection procedures, introducing an Automated System for Customs Data (ASYCUDA) system for customs data collection, and reforming the duty drawback system.

A recent study in the Poverty Eradication Action Plan (2004) notes that local government's concern with revenue generation retards the growth of micro, small, and medium-size enterprises. It shows that local taxes on small businesses are highly regressive, cutting into profit margins by as much as 50 percent for the smallest businesses. Moreover, the revenue collected is not used to provide business relevant services.

No research appears to have been conducted on Ugandan women's experiences with taxes and customs. A report on firms' experience with corruption in Uganda highlighted the issue of bribery in relation to tax, but it did not disaggregate the data to enable comparisons between the experiences of men and women (Svensson 2001). There is compelling evidence that enterprises owned by women are subject to significantly more bribery and harassment than enterprises owned by men. The 2004 Uganda Regulatory Cost Survey Report found that while 25 percent of all enterprises reported that government officials had "interfered" with their business—by threatening to close it or asking for bribes, for example—43 percent of enterprises owned by women reported interference (Kirkpatrick and Lawson 2004). If bribery at the firm level indeed disproportionately affects women, policy interventions need to be designed to tackle the problem.

The URA has made only limited efforts to meet the needs of women taxpayers, who have less education, lower rates of literacy, and fewer formal business skills than men and therefore find dealing with the URA challenging. One businesswoman stated that she closed her shop every time the tax inspector visited because she did not understand how to keep her books properly (discussion during Doing Business 2004 Uganda Workshop, Kampala, February 2, 2004). Evidence from the Uganda Regulatory Cost Survey Report and pilot initiatives to reform the trade licensing system (see box 3.2) suggest that time-poor women find it difficult to comply with lengthy and time-consuming regulatory requirements. Uganda's procedures for tax registration with the URA are complex, requiring taxpayers to provide three separate numbers tax: a corporate income tax number, a pay as you earn number, and a VAT number. Although these lengthy and costly procedures affect all businesses, it is likely that the impact is greater for enterprises headed by women, because these businesses tend to be small, women have less time to spend on such matters, and women have less access to the resources needed to navigate their way through the system.

To deal with these problems, the URA should asses its relationship with women taxpayers, particularly business owners, as part of its ongoing reform program. It would be helpful, for example, if the issue were addressed in the URA Customers' Charter and women entrepreneurs were included in the ongoing program of tax clinics and open discussions with the business community in Kampala. Many women entrepreneurs and URA officials have suggested creating a women's desk to address problems faced by women entrepreneurs. In addition, there is a need for fundamental reform of the Local Government Act to ensure a transparent system for taxation of businesses by local authorities.

6

Sectoral Perspective on Administrative Barriers to Investment and Labor Laws

Nondiscriminatory treatment of workers of different sexes, races, or religions can be regarded as a worthy social goal in itself. The elimination of discrimination can also improve both efficiency and growth.
— Appleton, Hoddinott, and Krishman 1999

Uganda: Administrative Barriers to Investment Update (FIAS 2003) reviews the impediments to establishing and operating a business in sectors identified as priorities for strategic exports by the Government of Uganda: coffee, fish processing, and textiles and apparel.

Coffee is of tremendous importance to households in Uganda: 500,000 households depend on coffee as an important source of income. Women are rarely the beneficiaries of such income, however. Despite the fact that women contribute their labor to raising cash crops, men control the resulting income. This means that women may lack the incentive to increase production (World Bank 2005a).

Women constitute only 20 percent of employees in the formal sector (World Bank and Ministry of Gender and Community Development 1995), but they are significantly represented in both fish processing and garment factories. The 2003 FIAS report notes that there are 10 active fish plants employing 2,650 people, 34 percent of whom are women. The vast majority of garment factory workers are women.

The legal framework for factory employment—including health, safety, and labor standards—dates from colonial times. The regime is inappropriate for the modern workplace, and even the current regime is not effectively enforced. Both investors and employees would benefit from transparent and properly enforced labor standards. Research suggests that such standards can increase investment, leading to higher productivity and wages (DFID 2004).

Key employment issues that affect women in Uganda include discrimination in recruitment and retrenchment practices, sexual harassment in the workplace, maternity leave and pay, and specific anomalies, such as the prohibition on women working at night (see box 6.1). A recent ILO Gender Assessment notes, "There is discrimination among men and women at workplaces in Uganda. Women are discriminated against with respect to recruitment, advancement, promotion, training opportunities and dismissal or lay off at work places. This has restricted their participation in decision making at all levels" (ILO 2003).

More broadly, Uganda's legal framework for employment is clearly in need of modernization. As one observer notes, "Despite its post-independence date, [the Employment Decree] is based upon colonial master and servant legislation. It does not reflect modern concepts in regard to contracts of employment, discipline and certain conditions of work.... It also appears that many provisions of the Employment Decree are ignored in practice" (Dr. Napier, Cambridge University, in commentary on Employment Rights Bill prepared for Uganda).

Initiatives have been taken to reform labor standards in Uganda. In a growing number of developing economies with export-oriented industries,

---

Box 6.1. International Experience Reveals the Inefficiency of Gender Discrimination

A number of recent international studies demonstrate the economic inefficiency of gender discrimination. A study of Fortune 500 companies from 1990 to 1998 found a strong positive correlation between a company's profits and the number of senior women executives (Adler 2001). Another study found that companies with the highest percentage of women had a 35 percent higher total return on equity and a 34 percent higher total return to shareholders than companies with the lowest percentage (Catalyst 2004).

Discrimination against women has economywide effects. A recent study in India compared states in which cultural norms restricted women's participation in the workforce with more modern states. It found that a lower proportion of women in skilled and managerial positions correlated with lower economic growth (Esteve-Volart 2004). A 10 percent increase in the women-men ratio for managers in India is estimated to increase total per capita output by 2 percent.

market-focused corporate social responsibility systems are setting standards for enforcement. These efforts are responding to the increasing importance placed by international buyers on enforcement of appropriate labor standards and codes of conduct, such as the Calvert Women's Principles Global Code of Corporate Conduct. Cambodia is recognized as a world leader in leveraging good labor standards for commercial advantage in export (http://www.ifc.org/ifcext/economics.nsf/Content/CSR-IntroPage).

The Ministry of Gender, Labor and Social Development, with assistance from the ILO, has prepared four bills—the Employment Bill, the Labor Unions Bill, the Occupational Health and Safety Bill, and the Labor Disputes Bill—to comprehensively reform Uganda's employment laws. The standards in this proposed legislation are based on Uganda's Constitution, international conventions, and the ILO's fundamental principles of rights at work. Key features of the 2001 Employment Bill include the following:

- Discrimination in the workplace is banned.
- Sexual harassment in the workplace is banned.
- Up-to-date provisions concerning contracts of employment are provided.
- The rights and duties of employers are clearly set out, including the right to provide maternity leave and maternity pay.
- There are clear provisions regarding discipline, termination, and continuity of employment.

A few of the provisions in these bills have proved to be very controversial, largely because of concerns about their affordability and effect on investment. The proposal to increase paid maternity leave from 45 days to 12 weeks on full pay has proved to be particularly difficult. There is currently no legal requirement for private sector employers to make any provision for maternity pay during the statutory maternity leave. The Constitution provides that employers must protect women during pregnancy and after delivery. In practice, however, legal provisions on maternity leave are frequently not adhered to (ILO 2003). ILO best practice provides for a period of maternity leave of not less than 14 weeks, including 6 weeks' compulsory leave after childbirth (Clause 57 of the Employment Bill). The standard states that cash benefits should be paid during maternity leave, but in order to protect women in the labor market, such benefits shall be provided through compulsory social insurance or public funds (or in a manner determined by national law and practice). Given the current budgetary situation in Uganda, the low number of women in the formal private sector, and very high fertility rates, which threaten per capita income growth, the women consulted agreed that paid maternity leave was not a relevant priority for Uganda at this time and was acting as a hindrance to passage of more critical labor legislation.[1]

The private sector has legitimate concerns about the effect of proposed compulsory private sector–funded maternity pay (which is not in line with ILO's Convention 183 on Maternity Leave) on the economy as a whole and on the willingness of employers to hire women. An impasse over this issue appears to have halted progress on labor standards, which would benefit investors and workers (including women) alike. It is recommended that the government enact legislation to put in place realistic and affordable labor standards (including equal pay) that will not make employing women unaffordable. Realistic enforcement measures will need to be put in place. Urgent reform of the Factories Act and related legislation should be undertaken, and realistic health and safety standards should be enforced.

Note

1. Women taking maternity leave should not be penalized with regard to pensions. These issues need to be revisited once Uganda's fiscal situation improves.

7
Access to Justice

Legal, social, and economic rights provide an enabling environment in which women and men can participate productively in society, attain a basic quality of life, and take advantage of the new opportunities that development affords.
—World Bank 2001 (p. 115)

The constraints women face in knowing and enforcing their legal rights have already been highlighted, in relation to land and succession law, for example. Women in Uganda are also constrained in their ability to access commercial dispute resolution facilities. By international standards, enforcing a contract in Uganda is slow and costly (table 7.1). Women face particular barriers when trying to access justice. These include lack of physical access because of limited access to transport; inadequate training and orientation of court staff; culture, religion, and patriarchy; technical procedures; time poverty; and the inadequate representation of women throughout the justice system (table 7.2) (Government of Uganda 2002a).

Table 7.1. Cost of Enforcing a Contract in Selected Commonwealth Countries

Country	Time (days)	Cost (% of debt)
New Zealand	50	4.8
Botswana	154	24.8
Uganda	**209**	**22.3**
Tanzania	242	35.3
Kenya	360	41.3

Source: World Bank (2005a).
Note: Indicators reflect the cost of a hypothetical case of a payment dispute of more than 50 percent of income per capita in the countries' most populous city.

Table 7.2. Barriers to Justice Faced by Women in Uganda

Barrier to justice	Implications for women
Justice delivery agencies are dominated by men.	Male judges and court staff may have traditional attitudes and biases against women.
Physical access to justice delivery agencies is difficult.	The majority of women have neither the time nor the money to get to the justice delivery agencies.
Technical and nontechnical staff in justice delivery agencies lack gender training and orientation.	Staff in the justice delivery agencies are insensitive to gender issues and may hold gender biases that obstruct justice.
Financial and social barriers prevent women from accessing justice.	Most women are not able to afford a lawyer. Illiteracy is widespread among women, and women have fewer contacts in the public sphere.
Uganda's culture and patriarchal system uphold values that privilege men in the allocation of roles and resources.	These values and systems put women at a disadvantage.
Community-based dispute resolution forums are dominated by men.	Customary laws privilege men. Representation of women in community-based forums is very limited.
Poverty prevents women from seeking justice.	Women tend to be poorer than men and have less access to finance.

Reform Efforts

The Government of Uganda is taking forward a major program of reform in the Justice, Law and Order Sector, with budget support from a large number of donors. This program has two priorities: criminal justice reform and commercial justice reform. The first phase of the commercial justice reform program has ended. It had four components: reform of the commercial court, reform of the land and companies registry, commercial law reform, and reform of the legal profession. Of these, reform of the commercial court has been most successful.

Commercial Court reforms have been successful

The reform of Uganda's Commercial Court (a division of the High Court) is at the heart of the Commercial Justice Reform Program. The vision was for the Commercial Court to become a flagship for reform of the court system in Uganda. The remarkable successes achieved by the Commercial Court include reforming court procedures, clearing the case backlog, enhancing the use of mediation, instituting a customer service strategy, adopting output-orientated budgeting, and moving toward results-orientated management.

There is no evidence that the Commercial Court is perceived as gender biased—indeed, the tight scope of the issues it deals with makes it unlikely that there is scope for such bias (Forster 2004). The Commercial Court has an active User Committee, which includes women users.

In accordance with the original vision for the Commercial Court as a flagship for the rest of the Court system, the plan is now to roll out similar reforms to the other High Court Divisions and the Magistrates Courts. The effort is being spearheaded by the newly appointed Principal Judge, with the support of the Chief Justice.

Magistrates Courts and Local Council Courts Issues Need to Be Addressed

Reform of the Commercial Court has been a success, but the court is inaccessible to most businesses in Uganda. Magistrates Court are the most commonly used commercial dispute-resolution forum. The Justice, Law and Order Sector Gender Desk Review suggests that for most women, the Magistrates Courts are also largely inaccessible. Local Council Courts are perceived as more accessible (Government of Uganda 2002a). There are about 4,000 Local Council Courts set up at the local level explicitly to provide an alternative form of justice to the Magistrates Courts, which were perceived as corrupt and too expensive. These courts formally apply statutory law; but their deliberations are often guided by customary law, despite the provision in the Judicature Act that when customary law contravenes basic principles of equity or an existing statute it is not to prevail (Nordic Consulting Group1998).

A baseline survey of Local Council Courts established that these courts are perceived as accessible in physical and technical terms, affordable, user friendly, participatory, and effective, and their judgments are generally enforceable (Nordic Consulting Group 1998). Despite these generally favorable perceptions, concerns remain about the quality of justice dispensed, especially as far as women are concerned. There is evidence that users of Local Council Courts for commercial disputes would move to the formal court system if they could afford to do so (Law & Development Partnership and Steadman Research Services 2001) The Justice, Law and Order Sector Gender Review and the Local Council Court baseline survey suggest that the use of customary law may result in bias against women. Moreover, the baseline survey suggests that despite the requirement for women to sit on Local Council executive committees and thus on Local Council Courts, few women actually sit on these courts. The lack of women is attributed to the fact that the courts sit in the evenings or at appointed times for about four to five hours in a single sitting. Both the time of day and the amount of time required were thought to be a hindrance to women, who have significant domestic duties during these hours (Twinomugisha and Kibuka 1997).

Efforts are being made to address these concerns. Proposed amendments to the Resistance Councils and Committees (Judicial Powers Statute) 1988 provide for more gender-balanced and responsive Local Council Courts, and they increase the courts' jurisdiction. In addition, new operational guidelines for Local Council Court proceedings have been developed, tested, translated into local languages, and distributed. The guidelines cover human rights, ethical conduct, natural justice, and gender sensitivity. It will be important to keep the effectiveness of these guidelines under close review.

A key element of the Commercial Justice Reform Project has been to encourage alternative dispute resolution, in particular mediation, as an alternative to court proceedings. The focus of this effort has been the Center for Arbitration and Dispute Resolution (CADER), which is located in the same building as the Commercial Court and obtains most of its business through cases referred to it by the Court.[1] Most of CADER's mediators are women, which, CADER reports, has led to resistance to mediation from many in the business community.

A number of NGOs and other organizations in Uganda provide free legal advice and assistance through legal aid clinics and outreach programs, some of which are aimed specifically at women. These include the Ugandan Association of Women Lawyers (FIDA), the Legal Aid Clinic of the Law Development Center, and the Uganda Law Society Aid Clinic. In addition, the Ministry of Gender, Labor and Social Development has undertaken legal awareness activities for women, piloted a community-based paralegal program, and organized gender training materials for judicial officers.

Recommendations

Although promising measures are being taken to enhance women's access to justice, there is scope for further initiatives. Specific recommendations include the following:

- Adopt a policy that, say, 30 percent of the members of the User Committee of the Commercial Court be women. (Although the committee has female members, this is because they happen to be representatives of the organizations on the committee.)
- Have the Justice, Law and Order Sector Gender Working Group, which facilitates gender mainstreaming in the sector, take an active role in

developing the government's commercial justice reform agenda. Gender issues will be important with the new focus on Magistrates Courts.

- Building on the 1998 Baseline Survey of Local Council Courts, undertake follow-up monitoring and evaluation, in particular with respect to the effectiveness of the new gender guidelines.
- Enhance legal aid and paralegal projects, which tend to focus on providing advice and representation related to criminal matters, to provide accessible advice for businesswomen.
- Building on the civic education work undertaken through the Commercial Justice Reform Program and by NGOs, expand efforts to give women practical guidance about their rights and how to enforce them.
- Expand the useful work done by CADER in promoting mediation as an alternative form of commercial dispute resolution to link with the Local Council Court's role in determining commercial disputes. Mediation, with its focus on reconciliation and a nonadversarial approach, is in many ways akin to a customary justice approach. Currently, CADER's work is confined to Kampala, but there may be scope for the organization to take on an outreach role, working with Local Council Courts to train staff in mediation techniques for commercial dispute resolution.

Note

1. Since October 2003, 370 cases have been referred to CADER.

8

The Way Forward

Institutional Framework

The Ministry of Gender, Labor and Social Development plans, coordinates, and monitors the delivery of gender mainstreaming programs in Uganda. Its structures at the district and local government levels execute its mandate at the grassroots levels. The ministry spearheaded the development of the national gender policy in 1997. That policy is now being updated and revised to take account of emerging insights into the gender dimensions of poverty and development in Uganda and to build on opportunities afforded by new instruments and modalities for prioritizing and channeling interventions, notably the Poverty Eradication Action Plan.

The 2004/05 draft of the national gender policy articulates the centrality of the Poverty Eradication Action Plan as the principal element of the national planning framework within which gender mainstreaming efforts are to be implemented. The policy also recognizes that there are other relevant national policies and strategies, notably the Program for the Modernization of Agriculture, the National Agricultural Advisory Services, the Uganda Public-Private Partnership, and the Micro-Finance Outreach Plan. All of these programs have important roles to play in supporting the policy's overarching objective of eliminating gender inequalities as an integral part of Uganda's sustainable human development goals.

Collaboration among government ministries and between government and NGOs in addressing gender issues is well anchored in Uganda. The Poverty Eradication Action Plan Gender Group, established in 2002 under the leadership of the Minister of Finance, Planning and Economic Development, took the lead in coordinating and managing the integration of gender, as one of the key cross-cutting issues of the Poverty Eradication Action Plan. The Poverty Eradication Action Plan Gender Group is well placed to play a coordinating and oversight role in ensuring effective gender mainstreaming in implementing the various government policies aimed at promoting private enterprise.

The Minister of Finance, Planning and Economic Development has played a lead role in addressing gender issues relevant to its specific mandate, in particular by paying attention to gender dimensions of economic growth, including gender and equity budget guidelines in the Budget Circular for the 2005/06 financial year. Recently, the Uganda Public-Private Partnership process, also coordinated by the Minister of Finance, Planning and Economic Development, has sought to become more active in addressing gender issues. The World Bank–supported Private Sector Competitiveness Project, alongside the ongoing Poverty Reduction Support Credit program, is expected to help the ministry address such issues explicitly.

Other ministries have also been proactive in addressing gender issues. In 2002 the Justice, Law and Order Sector conducted a gender review, and the Ministry of Water, Land and Environment is beginning to tackle women's land rights and access to land. The Ministry of Gender, Labor and Social Development has a critical role to play in championing gender as a key issue for private sector development in Uganda. Its most important role in this respect will be to influence the design and implementation of the strategies and reform initiatives discussed above.

Entry Points for Reform

Ongoing Reform Processes Represent an Opportunity to Entrench Gender Issues

This assessment has made a number of recommendations for legal and administrative reforms for investment that have a gender perspective. Under the Poverty Eradication Action Plan, the government is undertaking a number of reform initiatives that represent real opportunities for taking these recommendations forward.

The Uganda Public-Private Partnership is the government's overarching program for private sector development in Uganda. The second phase of the strategy is currently being developed. This is an opportunity to ensure that the role of women in contributing to private sector–led growth is fully acknowledged and acted upon. A key issue will be to link with the Land Sector Strategic Plan to ensure that land reform that helps empower women is seen as central to Uganda's private sector development agenda.

The Commercial Justice Reform agenda (part of the Justice, Law and Order Sector) is in the framework of the Uganda Public-Private Partnership. It has made specific recommendations about commercial justice reform to ensure that women's voices are heard in the ongoing development and implementation of this agenda (see chapter 7). Recommendations to enhance women's access to commercial justice include effecting institutional reform of the Magistrates Courts, Local Council Courts, and the Companies Registry; increasing access to justice initiatives, such as training paralegals to focus on commercial dispute resolution for women; developing the role of CADER to enhance access to commercial justice for women; and developing gender-sensitive commercial justice performance indicators, including disaggregated statistics on a gender basis.

The government is developing Regulatory Impact Assessments (RIAs) as a key tool in policymaking. A draft Cabinet paper would introduce compulsory RIAs into the policy- and legislation-making process. With the Cabinet Office as a filter, the policy is for RIAs to provide an economic, environmental, and social assessment of the impact of proposed legislation or policy. This is clearly an opportunity to include gender as part of the assessment process. The draft Cabinet paper on the introduction of RIAs should make explicit reference to gender issues, and consideration of gender issues should be part of the regulatory impact analysis process.

The Ministry of Gender, Labor and Social Development Has a Key Role to Play

In its role of championing gender as a key issue for private sector development in Uganda, the Ministry of Gender, Labor and Social Development must focus attention on influencing the design and implementation of these initiatives. It is vital that the government enable women's voices to be heard directly in these processes, through women's active participation in public-private dialogue on private sector development issues. Women's participation should be seen in the context of the Fourth World Conference on Women in Beijing in 1995, where members of the United Nations made a commitment to "establish mechanisms and other forums to enable women entrepreneurs and women workers to contribute to the formulation of policies and programs being developed by economic ministries and financial institutions" (FWCW 1995, Strategic Objective F1.165(n)).

Uganda is the only country in Africa to have a woman on the President's Investor Council, designed to facilitate private sector input into policymaking at the highest level. This position should be institutionalized, based on the National Council for Women's Business Ownership model in the United States.

Women's Voice Needs to Be Heard in Policymaking

Providing the structures and entry points for women's voices to be heard is only half the story: women need to be strong and effective advocates in order to influence policy development. The Private Sector Foundation of Uganda, the key private sector representative body in Uganda, advocates on behalf of its members. But gender and growth issues rarely feature on the list of key concerns to be raised with policymakers.

The following recommendations are designed to enhance the ability of the foundation and other private sector organizations and NGOs to advocate effectively on gender issues and to have a real impact on policy development and implementation:

- Introduce and institutionalize a minimum 30 percent female representation on economic advisory as well as political decisionmaking bodies, such as the Uganda Public-Private Partnership committees.
- Institutionalize the position of a woman entrepreneur on the President's Investor Council.
- Enable the Council for the Economic Empowerment of Women in Africa to join the Inter-Institutional Committee on Trade.
- Explicitly reference gender in the Uganda Public-Private Partnership Strategic Plan, and ensure that monitoring and evaluation of the plan include gender-disaggregated data.
- Establish a Private Sector Foundation of Uganda Working Group on women's entrepreneurship to enable the PSFU to research and advocate more effectively on gender issues.

Appendix
Summary of Consultations with Women Entrepreneurs in Kampala, Uganda

On February 2, 2004, Dr. Maggie Kigozi, Director of the Uganda Investment Authority (UIA), hosted a workshop in Kampala for about 40 women entrepreneurs and female staff of the UIA. Representatives of the Chamber of Commerce, the Manufacturers Association, the Uganda Women Entrepreneurs Network (WEN),[1] and the Canadian and African Businesswomen's Alliance attended, along with representatives of both home-based and formal businesses of all sizes. Sectors included tourism, soft drink processing, funeral services, event planning, textiles, fashion design, music, horticulture, handicrafts, and manufacturing. Four journalists also attended the meeting.

The workshop was part of the presentations and consultations with women as input into the *Doing Business 2005* report. Participants stressed the different needs of rural women, poor women, and formal sector entrepreneurs. They identified the key issues facing women, including discriminatory provisions in property rights, which lock women into small, informal sector businesses; gender dimensions of access to finance; and the need for capacity building, business training, role models, networks, and access to markets.

By way of introduction, Dr. Kigozi explained that UIA's mandate is to focus both on new investment opportunities and existing investors in Uganda. She commented on the useful work FIAS had done on identifying and helping remove administrative barriers to investment but noted that gender issues had not been addressed. She indicated that the Minister of Finance would be interested in FIAS undertaking work on specific barriers to investment that women face and making recommendations on how these barriers might be mitigated to improve economic growth in Uganda.

Uganda's president has led a very successful program of affirmative action that has increased the representation of women at all levels of decisionmaking, from village councils through to boards and government bodies. (As Dr. Kigozi noted, the head of the Uganda Revenue Authority is also a woman.) Despite this progress, however, policymakers still do not take into account the significant contribution of women to the economy and the gender-specific barriers to business development women face.

Participants at the Kampala meeting identified several needs and developments affecting women in Uganda:

- Statistics that are disaggregated by gender are needed to ascertain the true levels of women's involvement in the private sector, in both the formal and informal economies.
- Property is a key issue for women in business. Traditionally, women have not been included on land title registrations, even if they contributed to the purchase. This lack of collateral means that they are unable to obtain business loans and are often frustrated in their attempts to expand their businesses.
- Access to finance is a major problem for Ugandan businesswomen. Interest rates are very high; obtaining financing for women's businesses, which are predominantly in the service sector, can be particularly problematic; and male bankers often discriminate against women. One woman recounted wanting to expand her successful manufacturing business into the export sector. Together with a businessman who owned a similar but smaller and less successful business, she approached a bank to inquire about a loan. The banker paid attention only to the man, virtually ignoring her. Despondent over her experience, she put off the idea of exporting. Other women have had similar experiences.
- Microfinance is perceived as a very valuable service for women, who are recognized as better payers in Uganda and hence have easier access to microcredit. The Micro Deposit Taking Institutions Bill was passed in 2002, and the industry is becoming less NGO–based and more viable as a business service.
- The group loan mechanism in microfinance helps mitigate the property ownership/collateral issues faced by women. But the higher interest rates and short-term loan approach of microfinance institutions means that women are often trapped in the informal sector, unable to expand their businesses.
- Creating a credit registry would help women benefit from their good credit histories.
- More women are needed in the banking sector. Currently, women hold only the lowest positions at banks, without any decisionmaking power. More women credit officers could improve the situation for women entrepreneurs.
- There is a huge need for capacity building in corporate governance and basic business skills (business planning, finance, tax and audit issues, management). UIA is running weekly two-hour evening seminars on

key business topics, such as how to start a business, to audiences of 300–500 people. The demand for in-depth training is enormous.

- The need for training for women is especially acute, as they are less likely to have role models, be encouraged to go into business, have as much education as men, or take risks if they do not know what the outcome is likely to be. They are also likely to be uncertain of business basics. One woman, for example, said she closes her shop every time the tax inspector visits, because she doesn't understand how to keep her books properly.

- Perceptions of corruption are still rife, even though the reality has changed. People need to be convinced that business inspections are well run and that bribes are not extracted, so that they will be more willing to invest. People also need to know that they can obtain jobs on their own merits.

- The mindset of both the general public and girls and women themselves needs to be changed about women's ability to run and expand successful businesses. Self- esteem is an issue. Dr. Kigozi noted that there is a pilot project to encourage entrepreneurship in schools, which could include a gender dimension.

- Women's private sector issues can be divided into three distinct groupings: the educated elite, poor women, and rural/village women. As the issues they face are quite different, a targeted approach to their problems will be most successful.

- More women than men are involved in farming, but most of them work in the informal sector. Women are more likely to use their income to improve the lives of their the family, paying school fees for children, and so forth. Women with the ability to earn income are good for families.

- Labor laws in Uganda prevent discrimination and are designed to protect the vulnerable. Young girls must now go to school, and the authorities will intervene if they find young girls working.

- Government workers on maternity leave receive full pay for three months. In the private sector, paid maternity leave is voluntary (if the private sector were required by law to match government conditions, employers would be reluctant to hire women).

- Childcare is not an issue for working women in the formal sector in Uganda because of the wide availability of very inexpensive domestic assistance. Childcare is not deemed to impede women's participation in business, even for poor women, due to extended families and social mores.

- Polygamy is not legal, but it is accepted in practice. This can have adverse effects on women in terms of security of land tenure and inheritance. The government is now addressing these issues through the Domestic Relations Bill, under which a wife is entitled to a quarter of the family land

and children have a set inheritance, which can be claimed through the government.

- Women need to be connected with businesswomen in other countries. It is very expensive to travel, but often that is the best way to understand potential new markets and make the right contacts.
- Building trade capacity—understanding the opportunities, the context of international trade agreements, and the practicalities of export and how to access markets and develop networks—is key for women entrepreneurs with larger businesses.
- Most World Bank programs for women seem to involve the rural sector. The Bank needs to help women entrepreneurs who are ready to expand their businesses and create more jobs.
- Women's voices from the private sector need to be heard at the World Bank, as well as within both the government and the opposition, to ensure that women's views are taken into account in economic policy-making and private sector development.

Note

1. The Women Entrepreneurs Network (WEN) was created in 2001, when the UIA realized that women were not attending its events and needed an association that better met their needs. The WEN is now a vibrant network whose activities include mentoring, capacity building, cross-selling, and business referrals. To help create awareness of the role women are playing in investment in Uganda, the WEN sponsors an annual awards program and selects a distinguished woman investor of the year.

References

Adler, Roy. 2001. "Women in the Executive Suite Correlate to High Profits." Glass Ceiling Research Center, Malibu, CA.

Akello, G. 2001. "Women's Role in Agricultural and Rural Development: The Socio-Economic Condition." In *Summary Report of the Seminar "Strengthening the Economic Role of Women in Agriculture and Rural Development by Revisiting the Legal Environment."* Kampala: Centre for Agricultural and Rural Cooperation.

Appleton, Simon. 1996. "Women-Headed Households and Household Welfare: An Empirical Deconstruction for Uganda." *World Development* 24 (12): 1811–27.

Appleton, Simon, John Hoddinott, and Pramila Krishnan. 1999. "The Gender Wage Gap in Three African Countries." *Economic Development and Cultural Change* 47 (2): 117–54.

Asiimwe, Jacqueline. 2002. "Women and the Struggle for Land in Uganda." In *The Women's Movement in Uganda: History, Challenges and Prospects,* eds. A.M. Tripp and J.C. Kwesiga, 119–37. East Lansing, MI: Michigan State University Press.

Baden, Sally. 1996. "Gender Issues in Financial Liberalisation and Financial Sector Reform." Institute of Development Studies, Sussex, United Kingdom.

Banenya, Sarah. 2002. "Gender and the Administration of Justice." Report on Workshop on Commercial Justice for Investment Promotion in Uganda, July 29–31.

Barwell, Ian. 1996. "Transport and the Village: Findings from African Village-Level Travel and Transport Surveys and Related Studies." World Bank Discussion Paper No. 344, Africa Region Series, Washington, DC.

Blackden, C. Mark. 2004. "Gender and Energy in Uganda: A Brief Summary of Issues for the PEAP Revision." World Bank, Washington, DC.

Blackden, C. Mark, and Chitra Bhanu. 1999. "Gender, Growth, and Poverty Reduction. Special Program of Assistance for Africa 1998 Status Report on Poverty." World Bank Technical Paper No. 428, Washington DC.

Blackden, C. Mark, and Elizabeth Morris-Hughes. 1993. "Paradigm Postponed: Gender and Economic Adjustment in Sub-Saharan Africa." Technical Note No. 13, World Bank, Africa Region, Poverty and Human Resources Division, Technical Department, Washington, DC.

Booth, David, Deborah Kasente, George Mavrotas, Gloria Mugambe, and Abdu Muwonge. 2003. *Ex Ante Poverty and Social Impact Analysis: Uganda Demonstration Exercise*. April. Kampala: Department for International Development and Ministry of Finance, Planning and Economic Development.

Canagarajah, Sudharshan, C. Newman, and R. Bhattamishra. 2001. "Nonfarm Income, Gender, and Inequality: Evidence from Rural Ghana and Uganda." *Food Policy* 26 (4): 405–20.

Catalyst. 2004. *The Bottom Line: Connecting Corporate Performance and Gender Diversity*. New York.

Christensen, Anne. 2004. "Gender Analysis of Uganda Household Survey Data, 1992–2003." Background analysis prepared for the World Bank Uganda Poverty Assessment, December.

Cleaver, Kevin M., and Goetz A. Schreiber. 1994. *Reversing the Spiral: The Population, Agriculture, Environment Nexus in Sub-Saharan Africa*. Directions in Development Series. Washington, DC: World Bank.

Deininger, Klaus, and Rafaella Castagnini. 2002. "Incidence and Impact of Land Conflict in Uganda." Policy Research Working Paper 3248,World Bank, Washington, DC.

DFID (Department for International Development). 2004. "Labor Standards and Poverty Reduction." DFID Policy Paper, London.

Dollar, David, and Roberta Gatti. 1999. "Gender Inequality, Income, and Growth: Are Good Times Good for Women?" Development Research Group, Gender and Development Working Paper Series No.1, World Bank, Washington, DC.

EBRD (European Bank for Reconstruction and Development). 1994. "Model Law on Secured Transactions." London.

The Economist. 1999. "1811 Limited Liability Is Born." Special Edition. December 23.

Elson, Diane, and Barbara Evers. 1997. "Gender-Aware Country Economic Reports." Working Paper No. 2, Uganda. Task Force on Programme Aid and Other Forms of Economic Policy–Related Assistance. University of Manchester, United Kingdom.

Esteve-Volart, B. 2004. "Gender Discrimination and Economic Growth: Theory and Evidence from India." *STICERD Development Economics Papers* 42, Suntory and Toyota International Centres for Economics and Related Disciplines, London School of Economics.

FIAS (Foreign Investment Advisory Service). 2003. *Uganda: Administrative Barriers to Investment Update*. Washington, DC: FIAS.

Forster, Stuart. 2004. "Commercial Court Management Adviser. The Commercial Court." Kampala.

FWCW (Fourth World Conference on Women). 1995. "FWCW Platform for Action, Women and the Economy, Strategic Objective F1.165(n)." Available at http://www.un.org/womenwatch/daw/beijing/platform/economy.htm.

Gelb, Alan H. 2000. *Can Africa Claim the 21st Century? World Bank.* Washington, DC: World Bank.

———. 2001. "Gender and Growth: Africa's Missed Potential." Findings No. 197, World Bank, Africa Region, Washington, DC.

Glick, Peter, Rumk Saha, and Stephen D. Younger. 2004. "Integrating Gender into Benefit Incidence and Demand Analysis." Food and Nutrition Policy Program, Cornell University, Ithaca, New York.

Global Entrepreneurship Monitor. 2003. "GEM Uganda 2003 Executive Report." Makerere University Business School, Kampala.

Government of Uganda. 1999. *Action Plan on Women.* Kampala: Ministry of Gender, Labor and Social Development.

———. 2001. *Land Sector Strategic Plan.* Kampala: Ministry of Water, Lands, and Environment.

———. 2002a. *Justice, Law and Order Sector: A Desk Review of Gender and Access to Justice in Uganda.* Kampala: Ministry of Justice.

———. 2002b. *Report on the Uganda Business Register, 2002/2002.* Kampala: Uganda Bureau of Statistics,

———. 2003a. *Country Status Report on the Government of Uganda's Implementation of the Beijing Platform for Action (1995) and the Outcome of the 23rd Special Session of the General Assembly.* Kampala: Government of Uganda.

———. 2003b. "Information Paper on Changes in Poverty in Uganda 1999/2000–2002/03." Paper submitted to the Ministry of Finance, Planning and Economic Development, October, Kampala.

———. 2004a. *Country Status Report on the Government of Uganda's Implementation of the Beijing Platform for Action (1995) and the Outcome of the 23rd Special Session of the General Assembly (2000).* March. Kampala: Ministry of Gender, Labour and Social Development.

———. 2004b. *Issues Paper for the National Land Policy.* Kampala: Ministry of Water, Land and Environment.

———. 2004c. *Poverty Eradication Action Plan 2004/5–2007/8.* Kampala: Minister of Finance, Planning and Economic Development.

Gower, LCB, D.D. Prentice, and B.G. Pettet. 1979. *Gower's Principles of Modern Company Law,* 4th ed. London: Stevens & Sons.

Gupta, Geeta Rao. 2000. "Gender, Sexuality, and HIV/AIDS: The What, the Why, and the How." Plenary address, Thirteenth International AIDS Conference, Durban, South Africa, July 12.

Gwatlun, D., S. Rutstein, K. Johnson, E.A. Suliman, and A. Wagstaff. 2004. *Socioeconomic Differences in Health, Nutrition, and Population*. Washington, DC: World Bank.

Human Rights Watch. 2003a. "Double Standards: Women's Property Rights Violations in Kenya." March, New York.

——. 2003b. "Just Die Quietly: Domestic Violence and Women's Vulnerability to HIV in Uganda." August, New York.

ILO (International Labour Office). 2003. *Project on Enhancing the Gender Mainstreaming Capacity of the ILO Constituents in Uganda: A Guide for Mainstreaming Gender and Decent Work Issues in the World of Work*. Geneva: ILO.

Kasente, Deborah, Matthew Lockwood, Jessica Vivian, and Ann Whitehead. 2002. "Gender and the Expansion of Non-Traditional Agricultural Exports in Uganda." In *Shifting Burdens, Gender and Agrarian Change under Neoliberalism*, ed. Shahra Razavi. United Nations Research Institute for Social Development. Bloomfield, CT: Kumarian Press.

Keller, Bonnie. 2003. "Engendering Uganda's Poverty Eradication Initiatives: A Desk Review on Gender and Poverty." May. Ministry of Gender, Labour, and Social Development and Ministry of Finance, Planning, and Economic Development, Kampala.

Kirkpatrick, Colin, and David Lawson. 2004. "Uganda Regulatory Cost Survey Report." Center on Regulation and Competition, University of Manchester, United Kingdom.

Klasen, Stephan. 1998. "Gender Inequality and Growth in Sub-Saharan Africa: Some Preliminary Findings." Background paper prepared for "Gender, Growth, and Poverty Reduction. Special Program of Assistance for Africa 1998 Status Report on Poverty." World Bank Technical Paper No. 428, Washington DC.

——. 2004a. "Gender and Growth in Uganda: Some Preliminary Findings and Policy Issues." Report prepared for the World Bank and Ministry of Finance, Planning and Economic Development. Draft Report for DFID Uganda, Kampala.

——. 2004b. "Population Growth, (per Capita) Economic Growth, and Poverty Reduction in Uganda: A Brief Summary of Theory and Evidence." February. Paper prepared for World Bank and the Ministry of Finance, Planning and Economic Development.

Kwesiga, Joy. 2003. "Review of the 2005 Gender Parity Millennium Development Goal in Uganda and Proposed Strategies for Achieving this Target." Department of Women and Gender Studies, Makerere University, Kampala.

Law and Development Partnership. Ltd., and Steadman Research Services. 2002. "Uganda Commercial Justice Baseline Survey." Uganda Commercial Justice Reform Programme, London.

Lawson, David. 2003. "Gender Analysis of the Ugandan National Household Surveys, 1992–2003." Draft report prepared for the revision of the Poverty Eradication Action Plan, October.

Lubega, Sarah. 2000. "Law Reform and Effective Implementation as the Means to Economically Empower the Ugandan Woman." Georgetown University Law Center, Washington, DC.

Malmberg-Calvo, Christina. 1994. "Case Study on the Role of Women in Rural Transport: Access of Women to Domestic Facilities." Sub-Saharan Africa Transport Policy Program, Working Paper No. 11, World Bank and Economic Commission for Africa, Washington, DC.

Moncrieffe, Joy. 2003. "Gender Review of Uganda's Sector PEAP Revision Papers." Ministry of Finance, Planning and Economic Development, Kampala and Department for International Development, London.

Mpuga, Paul, and Canagarajah, Sudharshan. 2004. "Are Government Budgets Becoming Pro-Poor? An Analysis of Social Services Delivery Trends in Uganda." Kampala.

Muhereza, Frank. 2001. "Ranches Restructuring and Changing Gender Relations in Pastoral Households in the Former Ankole Ranching Scheme." Centre for Basic Research Working Paper, Kampala.

Muntemba, Shimwaayi, and C. Mark Blackden. 2001. "Gender and Poverty in Africa." In *Faith in Development*, eds. D. Balshawe, R. Calderisi, and C. Sugden. Oxford: OCMS Publications.

———. 2002. "The Gender Dimensions of HIV/AIDS in Africa: Putting Gender into the MAP." AFTPM Technical Note, World Bank, Washington, DC.

Mukasa, Stella, Nite Tanzam, Hope Kabuchu, and Santa Vusia Kayonga. 2004. *Uganda: Poverty and Gender Assessment: Strengthening Linkages between Poverty and Gender Analysis in Uganda*. Copenhagen: Danish Development Cooperation.

NAADS (National Agricultural Advisory Services) Secretariat. 2003. "NAADS Poverty and Gender Strategy for the Delivery of Improved Agricultural Advisory Services." Kampala.

Nordic Consulting Group. 1998. "A Baseline Survey on the Operations of Local Council Courts." Danida Judiciary Program, Kampala.

OECD (Organisation for Economic Co-operation and Development). 2001. *Women Entrepreneurs in SME: Realising the Benefits of Globalization and the Knowledge-Based Economy*. Paris: OECD.

Snyder, Margaret. 2000. *Women in African Economies: From Burning Sun to Boardroom. Business Ventures and Investment Patterns of 74 Ugandan Women*. Kampala: Fountain Publishers, Ltd.

STD/AIDS Control Programme. 2003. *STD/HIV/AIDS Surveillance Report*. Kampala: Ministry of Health.

Svensson, Jakob. 2001. "Uganda: The Cost of Doing Business: Firms' Experience with Corruption in Uganda." Report prepared for the

Consultative Group Meeting, Kampala, May. Africa Region Working Paper Series, World Bank, Washington, DC.

Tanzam, Nite. 2003. "Affirmative Action in Ugandan Politics." In *Women's Political Space: The Experience of Affirmative Action in Eritrea, Tanzania and Uganda.* London: British Council and Department for International Development.

Tripp, A.M., and J.C. Kwesiga, eds. 2002. *The Women's Movement in Uganda: History, Challenges, and Prospects.* East Lansing, MI: Michigan State University Press.

Twinomugisha, N., and E.P. Kibuka. 1997. "Good Governance and Easing Social Tensions in Uganda: Studies of Operations and Justice of Local Councils." United Nations Development Programme, New York.

Udry, Christopher, John Hoddinott, Harold Alderman, and Lawrence Haddad. 1995. "Gender Differentials in Farm Productivity: Implications for Household Efficiency and Agricultural Policy." *Food Policy* 20 (5): 407–23.

Uganda Bureau of Statistics. 2000. *Uganda National Household Survey 1999/2000. Report on the Socio-Economic Survey.* Entebbe: UBS.

———. 2003. *Report on the Uganda Business Register, 2001/2002.* Directorate of Business Industry, Agriculture and Energy Statistics. Kampala: UBS.

UMACIS (Uganda Manufacturing Association Consultancy and Information). 2000. "Uganda Regulatory Cost Survey Report." Report prepared for the Uganda Deregulation Project, Kampala.

———. 2003. "An Impact Assessment of the Pilot Streamlined Trade Licensing Process in Entebbe Municipality (May 2002–July 2003)." Report prepared for the Uganda Deregulation Project, Kampala.

UN Millennium Project. 2005. "Investing in People: A Practical Plan to Achieve the Millennium Development Goals." New York.

UNAIDS. 2004. *Facing the Future Together. Report of the United Nations Secretary General's Task Force on Women, Girls, and HIV/AIDS in Southern Africa.* UNAIDS, United Nations Children's Fund, United Nations Development Fund for Women, and United Nations Population Fund, Pretoria, South Africa.

UNIFEM (United Nations Development Fund for Women). 2002. *Gender Budget Initiatives: Strategies, Concepts, and Experiences.* Papers from a high-level international conference on "Strengthening Economic and Financial Governance through Gender Responsive Budgeting," held in Brussels, October 16–18. New York: UNIFEM.

UPPAP (Uganda Participatory Poverty Assessment Process). 2002. "Second Participatory Poverty Assessment Report, Deepening the Understanding of Poverty." Minister of Finance, Planning and Economic Development, Kampala.

WHO (World Health Organization). 2002. *World Report on Violence and Health.* Geneva: WHO.

World Bank. 1993. *Uganda: Growing Out of Poverty.* World Bank Country Study, Washington, DC: World Bank.

———. 2001. *Engendering Development through Gender Equality in Rights, Resources, and Voice.* World Bank Policy Research Report, Washington, DC.

———. 2004a. *African Development Indicators, 2004.* Washington DC: World Bank.

———. 2004b. "Improving Health Outcomes for the Poor in Uganda: Current Status and Implications for Health Sector Development." Report No. 29425-UG, Africa Region, Human Development I, Washington, DC.

———. 2004c. "Second Private Sector Competitiveness Project, Project Appraisal Document." Report No. 29639-UG, Africa Region, Private Sector Unit, Washington, DC.

———. 2005a. *Doing Business in 2005.* Washington, DC: World Bank.

———. 2005b. "Uganda: From Periphery to Center: A Strategic Country Gender Assessment." Poverty Reduction and Economic Management, Africa Region. Washington, DC.

World Bank, and Ministry of Gender and Community Development. 1995. "Report of Study on Legal Constraints to the Economic Empowerment of Women." Ministry of Gender and Community Development, Kampala.

Index